# ONE-SENTENCE STORIES

### An Anthology of Stories

### Told in a Single Sentence

Written by 43
## Amazing Authors
Compiled and Edited by
## Val Dumond
## Muddy Puddle Press

*One-Sentence Stories*
© 2017 Muddy Puddle Press

ISBN: 978-0-9985489-1-3

Printed in the United States of America

Muddy Puddle Press
P O Box 97124
Lakewood WA 98497

Cover created by Strange Design
(strangedesigndk@outlook.com)

# Grammar Groping
## by Gail Ghael

the strong burly adjective
stretched out his dangling arm
and pulled the wideeyed noun
into his sentence

i want to hyphenate you
he whispered

oh no
came the reply
im a proper noun

not for long
he replied
as he proceeded to modify her

perfect grammar
said the gratified adjective

yes it was complete
agreed the contented noun

but she added
you should have used some punctuation

# CONTENTS

The Fun of Writing Run-on Sentences ..................vii
The Main Street Laundromat Massacre..................1
Professional Help..................2
The Condemned Widow Diet..................3
Daybreak ..................4
Boots on the Ground..................5
Conversations..................6
Did You Hear the News?..................7
Tennis Anyone? ..................8
Departures..................9
Holiday Greetings..................10
The Day I Was Born..................11
I'm Falling ..................12
The Man Who Dialed the Wrong Number,
    Accidentally Setting off a Chain of
    Events Resulting in the Nuclear
    Destruction of the Planet..................13
The Toughest Job You'll Ever Love..................14
Plastic for the Cat..................15
Dottie's Teenage Sons..................16
New Year's Letter..................17
Cajun Folklore, CFL101, Section 02 ..................18
The Vacuum Cleaner..................19
It's Gotta Be Delicious in My Mouth..................20
This is Love ..................21
I Forgot ..................22
City(?) on the Hill..................23
A Sole Shade of Gray..................24
Loreen Tells You How to Get Away with It ..........25
Lady in a Bank..................26
A Trump Sentence..................27
Yam, Oh Heart, Yam ..................28

20<sup>th</sup> Reunion — Class of 1968......................29

Scented Memories.....................................30

Discord in the Ascendancy ......................31

And It Is Called Life ................................32

The Whisper ............................................33

Connections ............................................34

Frustration:

      Who is Watching the Computers? ......35

A Literary Tragedy..................................37

You've Got This ......................................39

A Mother's Sacrifice ...............................41

the sound of snow ...................................43

The Middle of the Night..........................45

Black Umbrellas .....................................47

The Old Woman .....................................49

Make Your Pet a Celebrity ......................51

Motivation..............................................53

Deceit......................................................55

Closing the Red Door..............................57

E.C.U. .....................................................59

A Sentence is. . . .....................................61

The Handsome Man.................................63

Missing Car Dreams................................65

Baggage ..................................................67

The Strange Death at Poinciana House....69

A Stranger in the Village ........................71

Death Comes Calling ..............................73

Blue Tarp Mania .....................................75

How Can You Call it Love When. . . ........77

All the Way from Tacoma to Tucson .......79

Hard Labor..............................................81

MAMA.....................................................83

Home is in the Heart...............................85

Let's Talk Bridge.....................................87

Just One Sentence ...................................89

Rumba.....................................................91

It's in the Bloodline ......................................93

Maddie and Tilly..........................................95

Dear Mr. Luccarelli ......................................97

Nigel's Gift ...................................................99

Need Help ...................................................103

Pooped ........................................................107

Spider ..........................................................109

Dotty's Boys ................................................113

The Oak .......................................................117

Taxi Dancers................................................121

Please Just Listen.........................................125

I Wish I'd Been Mrs. Noah Webster.............129

The Defendant..............................................133

Acid Reign ..................................................137

About the Authors.......................................143

# The Fun of Writing
# Run-on Sentences

Most teachers faint at even the whiff of a run-on sentence, but the smart ones are using one-sentence stories to teach word usage and sentence composition. The rest of us find a lot of fun in writing long, very long sentences and, in many cases telling a story in the process. All the while we've discovered this exercise is as relaxing as it is F-U-N.

The idea for writing a one-sentence story grew from a challenge unwittingly sent out by Harvard Professor Steven Pinker, PhD, who cited in his book, *The Language Instinct*, "the longest sentence" of 110 words, written by George Bernard Shaw. Twenty years later, Dr. Pinker upped the ante in his book, *The Sense of Style*, to the 340-word sentence he found in a novel. The challenge was on!

I sat down with a vague story idea and began what I would call a simple sentence with noun and verb, adding modifiers — adjectives, adverbs, clauses, and phrases — until I thought I had passed the 340 mark, only to learn I had almost 500 words. About the same time, I learned of a short story contest with a limit of 500 words, where I entered my one-sentence story, and won a prize!

When the idea of sharing this discovery took hold, I decided to try for an even longer story and took a couple of deep breaths before plunging into the keyboard. After a few tries, a story emerged from the drifting words, written without pauses for periods or semi-colons. There it was — a story in 1139 words, 853 longer than Dr. Pinker's latest example! The sky became the limit!

In the earlier reference to Shaw, Dr. Pinker was making the point of the "sheer vastness of language", adding, "Estimates of the number of sentences that an ordinary person is capable of producing are breathtaking". What followed was a discussion about sentence *length*, where he made it clear that any sentence can be made longer with just one word.

He wrote, "Indeed, if you put aside the fact that the days of our age are threescore and ten, each of us is capable of uttering an infinite number of different sentences. By the same logic that shows that there are an infinite number of integers — if you ever think you have the largest integer, just add 1 to it and you will have another — there must be an infinite number of sentences." (For more about sentences, read Chapter 4, "How Language Works" in *The Language Instinct*.)

While Dr. Pinker was unable to partake in this book project, he did think it a good idea, wished us well, and gave his permission to quote from his books where he discusses ways to diagram a sentence of great length — another of those valuable games that teachers offer students. By the way, that 340-word sentence from *The Sense of Style* came from one of the novels written by his wife, the noted author Rebecca Goldstein.

As a longtime word-doodler — journalist, leader of writing groups, editor of book-length manuscripts, and author of several grammar books — I immediately recognized the value of this kind of word-doodle. Not only is it fun, it challenges a writer to understand the parts of speech, sentence structure, and the guidelines of punctuation.

An unexpected value of writing long-sentence stories was pointed out by author Nick Page, who reminded me about the value of making every word count by using words sparingly. He wrote, "Every story has a beginning (*she wishes she hadn't jumped off that cliff*), a middle (*the air was chilly*) and the end (*thud*)". A short story in 23 words! Yes, the best writing makes every word count. But, it's stressful and more work.

A couple of writers drew me aside and explained how they used this one-sentence story process to help them get their story lines straight before beginning a novel. Other writers pointed out how you can write out a story idea in one long sentence, then break it down into parts: scenes or chapters that eventually lead to a novel.

Ah, the potential seems endless. But the best use of writing one-sentence stories, word-doodling, is the relief it offers to the stress of writers block, or the daily tension of work, career-building, school, child raising, dealing with a world on edge, the natural anxiety of holidays, upcoming exams, even waiting in a dentist's office.

For sheer fun — the *run-away-and-forget-daily-woes* kind of fun — you can't beat word-doodling a one-sentence story. Submit yours to Muddy Puddle Press, P O Box 97124, Lakewood WA to show up in the next *One-Sentence Stories* book.

—Val Dumond
Muddy Puddle Press

*[These 77 stories are listed according to the number of words, indicated at the end of each story, all the way from 101 to 1431, and please note that most of the stories can be extended even further...]*

# The Main Street Laundromat Massacre
## by Lucieno Marano

S IX WASHING MACHINES' WORTH OF SODDEN CLOTHES drifted lazily about, swirling, meeting, and passing each other by in the current, and from somewhere off to his right the gushing torrent continued still, as Eugene, standing perfectly frozen, like a skinny boy-shaped lighthouse in a tepid, soapy sea now risen higher than the tops of his ratty Chuck Taylors, cast a nervous gaze around the otherwise empty, completely flooded laundromat and knew — was absolutely, positively, one-hundred-fifty percent certain — that his mother would never believe this had not been his fault, though it had totally, completely, unquestionably NOT been... sort of... (101)

# Professional Help
## by Nick Romeo

*T*HIS DOCTOR IS ON THE CUTTING EDGE OF SCIENCE and medicine so he can easily fix your eye twitch, irritable bowel, and limp, while providing you with laser-shooting retinas, rocket-propelled feet, and retractable wings, as I've seen his body of work, from reattached head and spinal column to transdermal weaponized implants with LEDs, and with his help you won't be a puny heap of DNA waste material, because you will become a cybernetic supreme specimen of perfection, so make an appointment with his super sexy cyborg secretary, who is also living proof of his skill, then you can have the ultimate robust high-tech healthy body… (107)

# The Condemned Widow Diet
## by Luciano Marano

*E*THEL STEPPED INTO THE WARM EMBRACE OF THE BAKERY, a petite frail old woman swimming in a threadbare wool coat (always a thrifty one, Ethel), leaving the morning chill behind — along with all the condescending doctors and their awful tests and gloomy news — to cast a sly gaze over the decadent pastries, luscious croissants, and sinful truffles, arranged in gleaming cases before her like so much high-priced jewelry, knowing that if she truly did have just six months to live that she would unabashedly and with no regrets, for the first time in her life, darn well have her cake and eat it too, as much as she wanted… (110)

# Daybreak
## by Allen Berry

*A*FTER AN ENDLESS WEEK OF FIGHTING, MAKING UP, discussing reasons to stay together, and to part over and over again ad-nauseam, when they drew no closer to a solution to the declining state of the their relationship, oblivious to everything else, even the nightly news that brought ever more dire predictions of the world's super powers, they eschewed society altogether and took a much needed hike to escape their tension, and at the summit of the small local mountain the lovers found a kind of détente, where in that beautiful elegant newfound peace, they gazed out at the horizon, the light cresting there, and one remarked on the beauty of the dawning sunrise, and the other quietly replied, "That's west, the sun rises in the east." (126)

# Boots on the Ground
## by Ruth Anderson

*F*OR DAYS THEY FACE THE CONSTANT RATTLE
    of a never-ending battle
between foes who can't reason
    why chaos rules the season,
but boots scattered on the ground
    don't make a sound,
cheeks pressed to earth
    evoke no mirth,
a pool of colored mud
    won't reveal the type of blood,
a wailing, keening scream
    issues not from a nightmare's dream,
a buddy takes a round,
    a thud the only sound,
the medic kneels,
    but no pulse he feels,
alas no orders to retreat,
    ensure tomorrow's repeat,
while the enemy owns the night
    and hell prevails til light,
yet day brings a brief calm
    that dries the sweaty palm,
hunger and thirst
    invade the brain first,
but now bombs that are falling
    their names are calling,
another day at war —
    what for? (132)

# Conversations
## by Roberto Carcache Flores

*A* SHY MAN ONCE WONDERED IF IT WAS POSSIBLE to live free of letters, postcards, messages, and even words, having become distraught, gradually so, without ever really minding his feelings, to the point where a vow of silence began to seem like a good idea, though he did not really believe in his self-control, especially in the presence of the few people he surrounded himself with, people who were more like him than they cared to admit and who were constantly reminded of this similitude, as if it were something the shy man could cling to whenever they left his company, and so he carried on, brooding in public places, opening doors, waiting for the opportunity to break his increasingly prolonged silences to say something along the lines of "I think we'll be all right." (136)

# Did you hear the news?
# (Lenny's finally dead)
## by Luciano Marano

*L*ENNY HAD BEEN DEAD FOR MORE THAN A WEEK and was admittedly not a pleasant sight lying there in a field of parched grass, baked and bloated under the pitiless July sun, when Lennburgh County Sheriff Sam Dandy finally received enough angry phone calls to incite him to begrudgingly drag his ample behind off his customary stool down at Kathy's Diner and out to Floyd Ericksen's farm to see about speeding up the arrangements for the county's most beloved citizen — the ancient giant tortoise for which it was named — and now toted behind his squad car in a trailer which held a large piano crate coated in somber black paint and adorned with many flowers, in which to collect and inter the icon's treasured remains, though where exactly that interring would take place, he had no idea… (139)

# Tennis Anyone?
## by Barbara Wyatt

*A*T THE FRIDAY TENNIS TOURNAMENT, with hundreds of players entered to compete, happenstance prevailed and there I was, facing my ex and his new fiancée pitted in a match against me, along with some random player the captain paired me with at the last minute, but I had my new two-handed backhand-top-spin stroke, which the Pro guaranteed would send all opponents scurrying, sprinting, and chasing after deep spinning winning shots, and that is exactly what it did, and most importantly, when the random player and I overwhelmed my ex and his new fiancée easily, I launched my fist into the air with pride, but my third finger accidentally (well no, not accidentally) slid out of the formation of the tight fist and proudly straightened higher all by itself and gestured a passing thought to my ex and his new fiancée… (141)

# Departures
## by Roberto Carcache Flores

*E*ACH BOARDING PASS AND TRAIN TICKET renewed my ability to say goodbye, to be able to look into the eyes of someone dear to me and say what was needed to be said without making false promises or expressing regret, for deep down there is no such thing as a final goodbye, even between two people living on opposite sides of the globe, between the living and the dead, or between the part I leave behind in these airports and train stations with the person I am today, because in the end a goodbye is just a greeting, a word, an encapsulation of dusk in our memories, and the best thing to do is to utter *goodbye* with a smile after a long embrace and continue onwards, gazing into a distant place in which we will meet again, be it here or somewhere new… (144)

# Holiday Greetings
## (Sung to the tune of "Imagine" by John Lennon)
### by Stanley Krippner, PhD

*I* RECALL FRIENDS AND FAMILY,
It's easy if I try, and
I recall all my guests
Arriving by sea and sky,
How I showed them sights
And kept their spirits high
    With film festivals and operas
    That brought me lots of joy
    So did all the stage plays
    And music concerts I enjoy,
And the work with students,
Which was quite hard to do,
But after many sessions
Each of them came through,
Writing dissertations
While at Saybrook U!
    The programs for dreamers,
    With results — there's only one —
    A Saybrook certificate
    That arrives when they are done,
And I recall my workshops
Working with one's dreams,
Many held in China
Or the Philippines,
Where I recall all the people
Sharing with their teams
    Because each was a dreamer
    Who was not the only one,
    For they all enjoyed their insights
    While having lots of fun. (147)

# The Day I Was Born
## by KaCe Whitacre

*T*HE DAY WAS COLD, SO FRIGID THE FOG WAS FROZEN, but the couple knew they had to get to Tonasket since Republic didn't have an obstetrics surgeon to help with the birth of their first child, and then the fuel line in their Model-T froze (the only time the car failed them) and Jim sat shivering as he began going over the movies he remembered seeing while in World War II, hoping any first-aid training he could remember would help, when he saw a car coming up fast from the back and, hoping he could flag them down, he hopped out of the car, but not until they passed did he see their brake lights flash on as they backed up, and that's when he recognized the occupants as two young men he had helped out of a snowdrift the day before, Christmas Day, and now here they were the only car to come along, and the young men pushed Jim and Dorothy all the way to Tonasket (about five miles) where their first child was born without further incident. (181)

# I'm Falling
## by Jim Teeters

W ITH ONLY ONE WISH I HAVE BEEN FALLING, falling to meet the woman in my dreams, a mermaid named Alana with whom I have dreamily conversed, swam with, even wet-kissed while lolling among the seaweed forests, then falling with the sensation of fear as one who trips on stairs, but only this time still downward faster and faster now waiting the end — that thump followed by death I expect to feel — but when will this end is my unanswered question, and what will death be like, pain morphed into great pleasure or some kind of nothingness, and can it be that this leap of faith off the high cliff above that dreamed-of familiar ocean beach will indeed lead me into the arms of a walking Alana as I've been promised by that old mysterious peddler and, as I open my eyes, is it true I see her walking the beach (no fishtail) and me floating now so slowly and the smile on her face, her outstretched arms, the beautiful body I've craved now mine — as I softly land, and we embrace... (186)

# The Man Who Dialed The Wrong Number, Accidentally Setting Off A Chain Of Events Resulting In The Nuclear Destruction Of The Planet
## by Nick Page

*H*IS DEATH WAS NOT THE WORST THING THAT HAPPENED to Quale that day, nor was his wife leaving him, nor his dog biting him, nor his house burning to the ground, nor his suicide note with many misspellings, nor the humiliation of his wife finding him in bed with their dog, nor his failed suicide attempt, nor his running out of the burning house naked after the explosion caused by the gas emitting from their old kitchen stove, nor his wife having second thoughts and saving him from an oncoming bus, nor the bus running her over, nor the bus driver backing up to see if he hit something and running him over, nor that his roommate in hell was a novelist, nor that his missing private part had been in their dog's mouth, nor that a neighbor's child had retrieved said part and asked her mother, "What's this?", nor that that mother had been cheating with Quale's wife, nor that Quale had written a blackmail note to her saying, "I no wat you did," nor the fact that he would never know the worst thing that had happened to him that day... (193)

# The Toughest Job You'll Ever Love
## by Perry Ann Porter

O NCE UPON A TIME A LADY FROM THE GREAT NORTHWEST near the Seattle area decided to join the Peace Corps to volunteer her services in a foreign country to share her knowledge and experiences with a different culture by holding educational workshops for teachers among the many schools located in the area that needed books for their libraries and where she traveled by local transportation, riding in buses and sugar-cane trucks and hitchhiking on the backs of pickups to do her shopping before returning to her two-room thatched hut, smiling as she waved to the many friends she had encountered while living in a small Mayan Spanish village where she discovered she loved and enjoyed her adventures so much she decided to extend her stay in the first country, making it three years before she ventured on to three more countries, volunteering as a Peace Corps Volunteer for a total of seven years, promoting world peace and friendship while living at the same level as the local people, experiencing the Toughest Job She'd Ever Love, following the encouragement from John F. Kennedy in 1960 as he established this expanding organization to live abroad, contributing to world peace... (197)

# Plastic for the Cat
## by Richard Silverman

*I*T WAS A BLEAK, GRAY DAY OF INTERMITTENT RAIN and snow when walking into a crowded suburban supermarket on a December afternoon was not only a warm, convenient drying-off shelter from the brutally cold weather, but also a most welcomed public social intercourse for a recently widowed lonely old man without any family (except for a beloved orange cat named Sunnyboy waiting at home on his owner's unmade bed) who was in no big hurry to select the menu for his solo meal that night as he circled around the accommodating parallel aisles, paying more attention to the throngs of diligent hungry faces looking up and down the well-stocked shelves than to the hundreds of assorted stacked food items beckoning to be purchased before their looming expiration dates, as he continued to meander aimlessly with "Jingle Bells" playing on the overhead sound system while his booted frigid feet and toes finally got warm and his hand-held basket got full enough to place on the purchasing counter and wait his turn in line to choose the second of the two toting choices the overly friendly, nose-pierced young woman cashier offered… because plastic is more practical for the disposal of pet waste than paper bags…
(204)

# Dottie's Teenage Sons
## by Nita Penfold

*T*EDDY AND GEORGE WEAR TIE-DYED SHIRTS and faded jeans bought at the mall with their mother Dottie's money, know the words to all the Grateful Dead songs, long for the days of the real radical, and dream of having been at Woodstock, when one day they are discussing the Kent State incident from their American history textbook when their mother's friend, Loreen, overhears and tells them about being in Kent during the massacre, working at the A & W Root Beer stand as a carhop, how she had to drive her hysterical roommate home to Akron after she just missed getting shot coming out of her class, and how the soldiers almost wouldn't let Loreen back into town because it was five minutes past curfew and talking about the tanks parked on corners, helicopters buzzing overhead all night, the phones blocked, the young soldiers posted everywhere, and how she lost her job because she looked like a student, as Teddy and George gape at Loreen as if she has sprouted horns suddenly, this mousy little woman sitting in their mother's kitchen, and that afternoon, George takes the spindly marijuana plants he has been secretly growing in the attic and flushes them one by one down the toilet... (207)

# New Year's Letter
## by Paul Jackson

W ELL, THE YEAR STARTED OUT PRETTY HECTIC, trying to get over all the details of a Christmas season and before that Thanksgiving, and the death of my sister in October with a trip back to Michigan to sort all my dad's files she had collected as executor and never did anything with, just store them and leave for someone else to take care of, then along comes my niece's wedding and some other family things, and my son's birthday with presents, along with, you know, more family stuff, and now some health issues of my own and a hospital visit and surgery for my wife, and the Quarterly that still hasn't been completed for the proof readers, nor have I started work for the online blog I write for, and it seems choir and band rehearsals may be too much to think about or even to practice for, so I'm not sure we will get totally through the first few months of the new year, because of course, we have to get our files ready for the IRS, and cope with the early Trump term to see how effective the blackmail from Russia will be, and I'm thinking of becoming an expat because… it now looks like a terrific idea! (210)

# Cajun Folklore, CFL10, Section 02
## by Jude Roy

*3 credit hours*
*John Babineaux, professor*
*Foreign Language Department*

D EAR PROFESSOR BABINEAUX, you told us that we should be proud of who we are, proud of what we have become, proud of our language, proud of our symbols, but *je suis Cajun*, and by God, I have seen the language disappear in classrooms designed to assimilate all little Cajun speakers into Americans, complete with capitalist heroes and ambitions, have seen lumber companies raze the great Atchafalya cypresses until all that is left of the *soi disant* Eternal Wood are a few lifeless logs buried deep under dark alluvial mud, have seen ancient moss-covered oaks fall in the name of Progress and Subdivision, where houses spring up from the Earth like cruel imitations of the Life they supplanted, have seen schools of fish float face up in our bayous that reek of unknown poisons and chemicals, have seen *Mardi Gras* become a parade of drunkenness and debauchery, have seen the Cajun and Zydeco music sell cars and fried chicken, have seen South Louisiana invaded by oil companies with steel derricks thick as trees on the horizon, have seen followers of the petrol dollar feed upon the Culture like buzzards on Carrion, have seen what we have become, Professor, and my Shame mocks my pride... (213)

# The Vacuum Cleaner
## by Carol Margot Nelson

S O I CALLED MY DAUGHTER TO TELL HER that my Hoover sweeper had bitten the dust and had been ceremoniously tossed out, to which she replied "you mean that nice little red one I gave you in 2005", and I said "no, you never gave me a nice little red sweeper vac, your brother did", and she said, no, she did, and we went back and forth for a while not resolving the question, so I called my son who was at a party at the time and asked him if he did or did not give me a nice little red vac in 2005, but that I returned it because it was very loud and scared my ex-cat, and he had no clue, but his friend, who was the host of the party asked him if he was speaking to his mom and what did she want, so my son told him I had Hoover trouble, and his friend in a generous mood said, "oh I have a nice little silver one with a brand new belt that she can have," and to make a long sentence longer, when I got home from the YMCA, there it stood in the middle of my beige kitchen linoleum floor, ready to go, so I fired her up… (216)

# It's Gotta Be Delicious
# In My Mouth
## by Richard Silverman

W HEN MY SOMETIMES TOO CHATTY but quite likable coworker peered over our shared cubicle wall to ask me to *name my favorite food* I had to pause several seconds and consider her unexpected question because I'm much more particular about the *quality* of the specific ingredients I eat (or at least how my own taste buds rate them) than I am about ranking my favorites in terms of food categories like lasagna, pasta, pizza, hamburgers, enchiladas, salmon, steak, and so on down the line of all the various meals I prefer because a simple medium-rare half-pound cheeseburger made with fresh extra-lean grass-fed ground beef (not frozen please) and a thin slice of Tillamook white cheddar on one of my wife's buttered homemade buns (unsalted organic butter please) with a splash of ketchup on the upper bun surface, a slice of raw red onion over the perfectly melted cheese and a dollop of real mayonnaise (no Miracle Whip please) spread lightly on the bread under the warm juicy meat would please my epicurean sensibilities much more than a perfect looking three-course meal from a not inexpensive franchise restaurant where they use cost-saving / taste-killing preservatives in many of their ingredients and WAY, WAY too much salt in most everything printed on their fancy fervently profit-focused menus... (218)

# This is Love!
## by Eleanor Grace Wagner

*B*ACK IN HIGH SCHOOL, THEY'D WALK TO HER HOUSE after his agile feet had helped him toss a ball into a hoop, carry it over a goal line, slide him across home base, or after they'd seen a movie or attended a dance, slowing down as they approached her home until they reached the darkened entryway where he'd press her quietly so as not to wake her parents and gently so as not to hurt her against the wall where he'd kiss her softly on her neck, her brow, her cheeks, and finally on her waiting mouth until she whispered it was time to go, or her mother turned on a light in the nearby kitchen, and he'd slowly walk out the door toward his home, sometimes into the evening heat of summer, sometimes into the welcome frigid air that accompanied snowfall, until the next time, and the next time, until now, fifty-some years later, his tired feet shuffle slowly down the hallway of his own home, holding tightly to the walker, his head lowered to watch his dragging feet until they reach the bedroom, where she waits to help him into bed before she joins him, tucking him in, and then kissing him tenderly, ever so lightly, on his neck, his brow, his cheeks, and then on his waiting mouth, always waiting… (223)

# I Forgot
## by Bonnie King

*I* FORGOT, BUT IT WASN'T INTENDED since I would never want to inflict pain on a good friend who taught me the beauty of writing and now I've done just that because of my poor memory which also caused me concern about the possibility of dementia and that led me to watch a medical video to see if I have symptoms I could use as an excuse for forgetting that my friend had spent hours editing a piece I had asked her to critique and, although I did use her edits, I then promptly forgot she had done so and in writing her a thank you note, I only acknowledged her work on part of the manuscript, which in turn brought up memories of other times in her life when she had been discounted and saw herself as a poor communicator and not one worthy of notice, so as one who likes to "fix" things and people, and without the excuse of dementia — I passed the memory test — my challenge now is to repair the relationship, remove my friend's pain, and turn the focus back to my forgetfulness, instead of her memories of emotional trauma, and the best I've been able to do so far, given the stress we've both endured this year, is to suggest we ask for unmerited, divine assistance, also known as grace…
(226)

# City(?) on the Hill
## by Michael Robbins

*T*HE TIP OF THE WASHINGTON MONUMENT projected from the waves like a monument to hubris from where Micah stood in the grass amid a circle of trees bracketed by an array of radio towers, trailed as he was by a cluster of refugees who'd followed him from Georgetown to this high point near Point Reno, coming at first in twos and then in families or groups that just grew as he marched forth, as if a purposeful stride signified that he actually knew where he was going, pausing with him only twice to cast a glance down at the former citadels of power in the capital mall that were only shadows beneath the waves, the same waters that had just swept away the stiff-necks who had denied that the changes were their fault, that their inaction over an entire century would somehow mitigate the vanishing of the coastlines, which hardly mattered at all now that change had become inevitable, and Micah huffed and puffed as he recovered from his climb, realizing that all they could do was the same thing that humans had always done in catastrophic times, and that was to adapt, so that some day this spot in the shadow of the sandstone water tower ahead rising like a child's fairy tale castle, well, that glade might one day be their new city on the hill… (228)

# A Sole Shade of Gray
## by Roxana Dapper

*I* 'M NOT LIKELY TO TEACH ANY USA ADULT STUDENT anything s/he doesn't want to learn because, as we know, adult folks just don't cozy up to stuff they have no interest in since, heck, even sex with someone you don't want to have sex with is at the very least — to any passing ear — interesting, but, to the untrained educator, a non-interested, self-professed grown-up learner is a challenge, a wannabe learner just waiting to wanna learn, don't ya know, and so the beat goes on to try to teach these precious American English post-high schoolers how to read and write in basic (we're talkin' basic / fundamental / bare-bones minimum / grades 5-8 stuff) Standard American English skills, when all the time they really just wanna talk on their cells or text gibberish to their pals who pretend to understand exactly what they mean, and to text using intellectually creative characters and abbreviation in which we mimic our pre-literate ancestors (with precision), whom we idolize and deify as surely as we dwell in post-literacy intellectual grayness, as we have collectively forgotten that the mastery of high-level literacy skills (a still relatively new Homo sapien technology) opens the Brain Doors to complex problem-solving skills, but now we have ghostwriters who pretend to function as merely post-Sophist writers who will do our writing for us — so why bother learning how to think? — and I wonder when the ghost-thinkers will (soon) arrive... (238)

# Loreen Tells You
# How To Get Away With It
### by Nita Penfold

Y OU FLY OUT OF BOSTON, SITTING ON THE RUNWAY for three hours because of severe thunderstorms, miss your connecting flight to Eugene and have to be put up in a hotel for the night in Seattle, Washington, then take the first flight out in the morning for Oregon to visit your pregnant daughter and her boyfriend who keeps you up until one in the morning telling you about his life and why he loves your daughter, and a few days later you rent a car and drive northeast for fourteen hours from Eugene, up through the mountains and over an eerie black crater that's as silent as you've ever heard the world, as silent as the end of civilization, as silent as death, then down through llama farms and even a trace of desert with wild sage and a coyote, through Lewiston, Idaho, that smells like the armpit of the universe, all the way to Moscow, Idaho, to visit your other daughter and her boyfriend who won't look you in the eye when he speaks to you, and two days later, when you're just driving out of town minding your own business — well maybe slightly over the speed limit — thinking about what a good time you've had and how different your daughters' boyfriends are, as different as your daughters themselves are, you just happen to run over your ex-husband and you are so startled you back up to see what happened... maybe only once... (244)

# Lady in a Bank
## by Jude Roy

MADAM YA, KINKY HAIR AS WHITE AND FLEECY as a cloud in God's blue heaven, copper-colored skin, smooth like freshly minted dollar bills, bosom large enough to comfort a world of problems, ageless as the building she lived in, an old bank edifice, where bricks made good walls, warm in winter, cool in summer, had always welcomed her son when he visited, the son who had run away at fifteen to make his fortune in Chicago where banks offered money not shelter, and she watched as he hooked up an eight millimeter projector, showed images on her brick wall of a middle-class black family, portraying infants growing up on celluloid, blinked with the light when he was done, wiped damp eyes as he packed up the projector and ran away again to a houseful of family she would never touch, and died as quietly as she lived, climbing into her bed, closing her eyes, and replaying the images of her celluloid family against her eyelids until blackness took over, and never saw her son when he flew in from Chicago, camera ready, recording wake and burial, playing it back once on a white wall in his suburban home to a family that would never touch her smooth black skin, would never rest their tired heads on her bosom, would never see the town tear down the old bank after it had long outgrown its worth, leaving nothing except a pile of dust and smooth copper-colored bricks picked over by scavengers, until only a scar remained. (256)

# A Trump Sentence
## by Richard Silverman

A S AN ASTONISHED, OUTRAGED, VERY DISTURBED United States citizen who is still having conceptual problems getting my mind around the idea of a "President Donald Trump", my first inclination is to bark out (with bugged eyes) about this self-absorbed, prickly billionaire's lack of governing experience and his immature, sexist, possibly very dangerous personality that shouldn't be anywhere near making nuclear warfare decisions, blah blah, blah… rather than to take a couple adult patriotic deep breaths and focus instead on the upside of what we still *do* have securely in place within our imbedded well-governing democratic system replete with its official, established checks and balances to insure all of us of our inalienable Constitutional rights regardless of how much The Donald can avoid his executive duties, disregard presidential protocol and bend the laws toward whatever best serves him, his vast international business interests, his political cronies, and also toward what benefits each of his ever-compliant family members and expanding multitude of "trump drones" hovering in obedient concentric circles around his expanding quasi-Hitler reach, while castigating anyone (and I mean *anyone*) who disagrees with or criticizes any of his opinions, edicts, legal history, recorded admissions of illegal sex acts against women, his appointments of several totally inexperienced cabinet members or even dares to speak out against his embarrassingly crude, bloviating American personality that is the laughing stock of high-minded intellectuality all over the world… as I am openly daring to object to… vehemently, unafraid… right here in the printed confines of my First Amendment *writer's rights, I sez to Mr. Bully Prez…* (263)

# Yam, Oh Heart, Yam
## by Josh Shortlidge

*M*Y SOUL GENTLY CHANTS "YAM" to caressingly awaken my suppressed heart chakra, calling it forth to regale me of my forgotten childhood, often quietly vacant, yet sometimes radiating the warmth heralded by angels, slowly fleshing out secreted tales of youth that I simply *must* regain, determined that the story will rise like a phoenix from neglected but eternal embers, teaching me in dribs and drabs (and hopefully in eventual torrents) at a pace that my tabernacle can physically withstand and spiritually embrace, telling me of treasure troves beyond my wildest dreams, of all that has passed into me, from whence my pure soul is springing joyfully into my waiting arms, confiding in me just how this fifty-six-year-old stalwart artist-come-database architect, this father of two and even of a third adopted from my late sister, this husband and romancer of my loveliest "Red Squirrel" delight, my soul comes forth as a vagabond woven lovingly into a divinely soft and warm cloak, which my being wears with honor into eternity, it hugging my still-erect shoulders during their quest to discover how I grow up from here and how I bloom into a leader of hearts, finding time to play energetically with my superbly loving brother, my encouragingly creative mother, my ever-loving though now deceased father, and my wide throng of great companions, all building mind-boggling contraptions to unlock yet undiscovered troves of hopes and dreams, for which the future patiently and expectantly awaits, with humble and rested mind, with body and spirit, planning to weave those hopes and dreams as lovely strokes of fancy into these very moments... Yam! (268)

# 20th Reunion — Class of 1968
## by Nita Penfold

*T*HE REVOLVING MIRRORED BALL CIRCLING ABOVE catches faces mesmerized by a slow-mo video replete with yellowed high school photos lined up on velvet, and Loreen sees tired eyes, the judge talking about his son, the seventeen-month-old terrorist, with a former cheerleader gone to fat, balding men clutching their drinks, some holding hands with their second or third wives, watching that damn video as if it were the best time they had in their lives and there never would be anything better, but Loreen, she who never went to any prom, is kicking off her heels and dancing in her bright flowered dress with the only other single who showed up, now assistant to the high school custodian, along with her best friend, Dottie who always was in trouble during English class for not staying on the assigned topic and who now appears on TV talk shows for the Chamber of Commerce, with her new husband, and that girl who used to pick her nose in class and who now is an aerospace engineer with her husband, all helping the twenty-something disc jockey who feels like a failure because he can't find the right music to push the dance buttons of all these other people still standing idly watching the video photos of themselves as the future homemakers of America, future farmers of America, future businessmen of America, past jocks and prom royalty of America who huddle inebriated, squeezing their money's worth out of this reunion of the living dead, and after a while, the dancers sneak next door to the party for the class of 1978 from a rival school, where everyone still rocks and they can dance in a crowd until the place closes… (287)

# Scented Memories
## by Babz Clough

*I* SMELLED THE PIPE LONG BEFORE I SAW HIM as the wind must have been drifting the scent down towards me, and then he appeared with two big dogs on leashes and a woolen cap pulled down over his head, but he was young, younger than my father was when I think about him, a pipe clamped between his front teeth, the teeth yellowed and worn into the same shape as the corn-cob pipe stem, and I smiled at the young man, wanting to hug him, follow him, just breathe next to him so that for one instant my dad would be back with me, but this young man didn't have the straight corn-cob pipe my dad favored as his was a softly curled pipe that drooped down near his chin a bit, but as I walked past him I kept sniffing the air, and as we continued to walk, I continued to sniff the air, trying to get that last faint scent of my father the way he was before he got sick and chemoed and frail, trying to catch him the way he was when I was young and he was building a boat in the backyard and smelled of pipe smoke and fresh lumber and man sweat, and as I walked on, I hoped the young man with his drooping pipe and eager dogs had a happier end than my father, that the young man would see his grandchildren grow up and live a fulfilling life, and not die before all this came to pass, but that at the end, he too would have someone like me holding his hand, praying for him, as he breathed his last and that his last breath would have a faint scent of pipe smoke. (296)

# Discord in the Ascendancy
## by Patrick Hanks

*L*ONG BEFORE LORD HUMPHREY GEORGE FREDERIC Dumond, a scion of the Protestant Ascendancy in the Emerald Isle, who came into this world as the fourteenth son, reputed to be illegitimate, of the Fourth Earl of Youghal, was elevated to the peerage of Ireland for services rendered during the Succession Crisis, taking the title of Lord Comeragh of McGillycuddy's Reeks, he realized that, on account of nothing more than a careless remark that he had made in adolescence to his good friend Dermod, and that had been intended to be merely jocular but that in the event turned out to be devastating in its effect on the relationship between utterer and referent, there was no way that he could escape being the target, and in all probability also the victim of the flagrant hostility and indeed violence of the young man who in happier times, during their teenage years, had been his boon companion, by name Dermod Taidgh O'Brien, who was a linear descendant of Murrough O'Brien, the 17th-century First Earl of Inchiquin and Sixth Baron Inchiquin, known to history as Murchadh na dTóiteán (Anglicized as "Murrough of the Conflagrations"), but history has a strange quality of unpredictability and so it turned out, for it was Dermod himself who became the victim, when one day he approached the great house lying at the foot of the hill and beside the stream that cascades merrily down from Ben Bulben with the intention of seeking relief for the desperate and starving villagers whose potato crops had failed for the third year in succession, he received, not the succour that he was altruistically seeking, but a rude dismissal from his former childhood friend's presence, following which he was pitchforked to death by the servile retainers of the man who was destined in later years to become Lord Comeragh... (304)

# And It Is Called Life
## by Nick Page

*I* AM THE OAK WHOSE LEAVES FALL BROWN down to the Earth from which I grew long ago from an acorn, a seed in rich soil made of my ancestors who are dead but alive in me and my acorns, rich in memory of all the stories told under my branches by hiding children, lost children who seek, young couples carving names in bark, old couples shedding like me, birds repeating their one-sentence stories over and over, beautiful all the same, and the equally beautiful repetition of sunrise to sunset to rise, to set, to fall, to winter, to spring, to summer, and as these stories weave like light, like darkness, like air through my leaves, I listen, a slow listening with fragments of a ten-year-old's tears, how no one loves her, how she grows lovable, returning with love and lover to share loving things, and she grows to raise a child of her own, showing her child the gnarly initials now part of me, and she grows old and I grow old and I am the Oak and I know I am Holy and life is Holy and all is Holy and I know that I too will become soil for some future oak, and the stories of the chatty birds, the songs of singing children, the loving embraces of young lovers, the tears at life's seeming end, and I know that life never really ends and every living child, song, whisper, lover, leaf, never really ends because we are proof that life never really ends as each seed is made of me, and I am each seed, and all stories are one story, and that there is no beginning, no middle, no end, and we all are knowing that life never really ends, that we are one unending story and it is called me and it is called Life… (312)

# The Whisper
## by Judy Ashley

*I*N THE BEGINNING HIS NARCISSISTIC PERSONALITY, his emotionally abusive behavior, and his crazy mind games were well camouflaged as he preyed upon her recently widowed vulnerability by sending her flowers, inundating her with surprises and fun dates as he taught her how to play rather than to work all the time, and while she loved the attention, the fun times, and having someone taking away her loneliness, her heart told her that this was going nowhere, that it was somehow not quite right but, unfortunately, her attempts to end the relationship were fruitless as he simply would not go away, and it wasn't long before she found herself planning a small wedding which seemed to elicit more anxiety than excitement even as she thought about the good times, his family whom she loved, financial security, and all the while confusing the present with the past and mixing in fears of the future but ignoring the tiny doubts, the little red flags that she did not consciously see nor fully comprehend, and when she slowly began to awaken on the morning of the Big Day, a tiny voice inside whispered gently, *do not do this,* but when fully awake, she said to herself, *it is too late,* so she took a valium and calmly walked down the aisle that afternoon not knowing that everything was about to quickly change, the fun would vanish, and she would begin an agonizing journey that would end several years later only when she listened to the inner voice softly whispering, *the truth will set you free,* and when she finally found the courage to confront the truth, the tiny whispers grew into a loud, bold voice, *it is time to take back your life — you are strong,* and her resolve could not be broken as she listened confidently, replying to herself, *I am free, I can do this* — and that is what whispers are for... (321)

# Connections
## by Paul Jackson

*I*T'S WEIRD HOW THINGS COME AROUND AND HIT YOU to the point of changing directions you might want to with activities, when you meet someone at a writers meeting and start telling war stories, and the other person says, "I remember doing something like that in Alaska, when were you there?" and your response is "1962" and his, "I was there then," and it turns out he remembers I was a timpanist with the Anchorage symphony and he needed a timpanist for the Renton community band, and I agreed to come play with his group if he would allow me some leeway, given I hadn't been playing timpani or percussion for some forty years, and it would be a stretch to think I could be ready by Christmas, never mind that at that time I was able to also join the Gateway band and play in several other ensembles, and how we recruited some musicians and also had our jazz band, and it was pretty hectic learning all the music for ensembles and choir, which eventually had me saying "Whoa," because I couldn't handle the cost even though I had lots of time in retirement to do these things, and now I'm still in a choir, two bands, and I edit two publications and write for those as well as a national online publication for libraries, as I wonder if I can make it this November with rehearsals and three Christmas concerts, moving timpani, setting up, getting to the venues in I-5 traffic and SR-512 and #410, and then tearing down and doing it all over again about three times a week when we also have to deal with Thanksgiving and our wedding anniversary and my 81st birthday, while meeting a monthly article deadline, all in the same month, so that it all just seems to be over the top and, while I may be in the rose patch, blessed with time and energy, I sometime wonder if I really have time to smell those roses, and if I did, could I? (342)

# Frustration: Who is Watching the Computers?
## by Paul Jackson

T HE OTHER DAY I HAD JUST RETURNED FROM MICHIGAN and my late sister's memorial open house at her large Victorian style home where we had around fifty people attend that included several family members, nephews with spouses and children, and my sister-in-law from my deceased brother's family, and all of this was going on with the need to get my bag back from the airport that seemed to dislike the scissors I had kept in the bag overnight at Customs/TSA and, of course, now that I was back at home I had to figure out how to pay two automatic payment items for auto insurance and phones/internet which for some reason were not automatic, while I deal with the fact that a check did not get posted although the machines did indeed cash it, causing much of my first day home spent on the phone and the computer getting things straightened out because Lord knows... the companies aren't going to do anything as "the computers are correct and therefore you owe us something, so if there is a problem it is yours not ours", much like the time I got a ticket and the Secretary of State of another state included the same ticket twice on its report to this national database of infractions, which then goes to the state were one lives and gets recorded, where your insurance company gets the information so they can charge you more if you have more than one ticket/violation, at which time you have to tell someone, in this case the court, that they've erred in recording this, for which they then have to send a letter revising the report to the Secretary of State who then *has* to look at the record and revise what they did erroneously and leave all of us wondering who is watching the computer information to see if *it* is correct, and especially with IA coming to bear, you end up wondering will they, the computers, learn to catch their own mistakes since regular human beings can't seem to get it... (345)

# A Literary Tragedy
## by Allen Berry

*T*HEY MET IN A GRADUATE ENGLISH COURSE, as frustrated poets and sociopaths often do, grad school being the last haven for the lost, the embittered, the cynical, and the socially maladjusted, and as you might expect, they hit it off quite quickly and spent many an afternoon discussing Flaubert and Hemingway and their ilk over coffee — dressed in black of course as was the standard uniform of the day and the major — believing they were destined, it seems, to be the best worst thing that happened to one another as they created metaphors and theoretical readings of the subtexts of one another's text messages, notes, half-finished hesitant sentences, and as they drew closer and closer to their cataclysmic relationship climax, he being the sort to make the grand gesture for love and she cynically searching for the hidden meanings that would deconstruct her independence that placed her squarely in the thrall of her oppressor, and so they rocked forth with all the good fortune of the Ancient Mariner on the stormy sea of love, a phrase they both agreed was clichéd and stagey in the worst sort of pedestrian clichéd-ness, and all the while he kept trying to overwhelm her with the finest tropes of Shakespearean, Courtly, and Romantic love, while she grew ever more paranoid seeking to maintain her agency as the feminist heroine, resistant to his oppressive scopophilia, yet drawing him ever closer through her resistance as he sought to colonize her, raising his flag on her virgin beach, to which she reacted by cementing her place as the abject even within the narrow confines of the English department, which of course drove him to distraction, causing him to increase his pursuit to Quixotic levels of artifice so that one night she agreed to meet him beneath the Willow Tree in the Ophelia garden, where she promptly slit his throat, and as she eased the razor back into its case, she said, "you always were a romantic — too bad— seeing as you were born in the post-modern era without the requisite paranoia that might have saved your life." (348)

# You've Got This
## by Jennifer Schneider

"YOU'VE GOT THIS, KEEP IT UP, ANOTHER DEEP BREATH, keeping breathing, now exhale, now inhale… yadda yadda yadda…", her coaching (or more appropriately, her orders) was coming at me at a fast and furious clip that more closely resembled a live auction at an auction house selling goods that no one wanted, but all I could do was try to breathe, and count, 10, 9, 8, 7, 6, 5, 4, 3, 2, 1 and again 10, 9, 8, 7, 6, 5, 4, 3, 2, 1 and I tried, I kept trying as I heard, "you've got this, you can do this, you will do this…" which I repeated to myself over and over, "just keep moving, keep going, you can get there (wherever *there* might be)", and if I can keep the words and numbers swirling in my head maybe I really *can* do this, maybe I really *will*, and all I could think of was the bounty of hydration, the satisfaction and the ultimate relief that awaited me at the finish line, so I persisted and continued to move one heavy block-like foot in front of the other and somehow, quite miraculously, I continued to push myself forward despite my aching body and tired mind's incessant cries for me to resist and preferably halt my forward motion, but somehow I continued and so did she intoning "You've got this, keep it up," as she continued to relentlessly remind me how close, but at the same time how far, I was from the end, the goal, but wait, suddenly I saw it, the crowds, the strong waving arms in sharp contrast to my flailing arms, the smiles, the ribbon — oh, that glorious red ribbon — and so I dug deep, I found new life in my otherwise lifeless soul and aching limbs and I charged, eager to experience the glory of finishing and then, I too smiled, not only for the relief, but also for the realization that deep within each of us lies the ability to accomplish whatever we put our minds to and for that I cheer, I celebrate, and I persist until it's time to reach for the water bottle… (364)

# A Mother's Sacrifice
## (From a dream 11-06-2010)
## by Diane H. Larson

*I* WATCHED THE BEAUTIFUL YOUNG WOMAN, her handsome lover, and the dark and wrinkled old woman as they focused on the girl in the bed, the young woman leaning down to hug her blind daughter and to whisper to her of the glorious new place they were going to live where the little girl would be able to enjoy the taste and smell of the salty sea air and feel the heat of the sun on her skin, and when the young mother pulled back, the glow of her deep love for her child spreading out in ever-widening circles, warming all within reach, she turned toward her lover, waiting patiently behind her, and gave a slight digging motion with her hands, a signal only he would recognize, her eyes meeting his gaze with such passionate intensity that smoldering coals burst into hot flames, causing the old woman, who was no longer able to feel such heat, her calcified senses having long blotted out the memory of such passion, to shake her head in despair as she watched them leave the room together, and later when the young woman came out of the room, smiling like a Cheshire cat, her adolescent son, passing in the hallway, caught the look on her face and smiled wickedly at her and cast a knowing glance in my direction, and as I watched from the top of the stairwell, the women and the girl, followed by the boy, though not the lover, descended the steep staircase and left their keys at the bottom of the stairs, the boy giving me one last glance and a jaunty nod before tossing his keys on top of the pile as I, for a moment, continued to stare down the long empty stairwell at the keys, and then with a resigned sigh, I turned and walked over to the front window, drew back the wispy lace curtain as I just had to see, and there they all were, sitting in a straight line in the back of an old pickup truck parked across the street, and on the side of the truck, I read the words I somehow knew would be printed there…"Department of Immigration". (366)

# the sound of snow
## by Babz Clough

A S I HIT SEVENTY-FIVE MILES AN HOUR on the interstate heading south into Boston, I could hear the frozen snow sloughing off my car, and all I could think was the sloughing off of people who I had met along the way, friends and ex-roommates and colleagues, people who were part of my old days and my past lives, and I thought how life was a sloughing off, even of sisters and brothers and people you were supposed to keep forever, and I tried to slough off the carefully worded conversations still unspoken that I should have had with my sister, the one who would send me random texts at five o'clock in the morning, to which I'd respond with an exquisitely crafted text that I spent an hour creating in an effort not to cause offense, not to say the wrong thing that would mean a silence of weeks or months or years, but then not getting any response to my exquisite crafting and realizing in the silence that something I had said or not said was the cause, but as the snow sloughed off the car I thought that maybe there was nothing I could have said or done or written that would have changed her response, even though she had initiated it, and I hated texting anyway for all the reasons everyone hates it, so as I sped down the highway, the vibration from the powerful engine a tympanic backdrop to the sloughing snow, I imagined I could hear the snow loosening, getting ready to let go, the friction of wind warming the skin of the car just enough to free the icy mass, but maybe not, maybe I just imagined I could hear it, but I know I heard loud and clear the slightly higher pitched sound, the whoosh of the snow as it slid along the curves of the car and then silence as it let go, and maybe it made a sound when it hit the highway at seventy-five miles an hour, but I was moving too fast to hear it, for I was already down the road, but then again, maybe it didn't make a sound, maybe it just dropped off, like the message from my sister, never to be heard from again, just a black puddle where once sparkling white snow used to be... (392)

# The Middle of the Night
## by Emily Jayne Milton

Y OU COULD CALL ME IN THE MIDDLE OF THE NIGHT and I
would answer and hear your voice call my name and I
would ask, Who is this? and you would answer with your sweet
name and I would laugh then and tell you that I was teasing,
that of course I know your voice, the voice I have heard for
years, decades, a lifetime, the voice that I would recognize if I
were swimming the Pacific all the way to China or cutting
through the ice of the frozen Arctic or dawdling among the
locals at a Paris café as I sip the rich Bordeaux that was our
favorite all those years, decades, lifetimes ago, and you would
smile because, even over a wireless wire I can hear your smile,
breathe in your scent, feel your soft hands caress my shoulders
the way you did all those years, decades, lifetimes ago, and we
can talk now about those brief moments, stolen from the
workday drudgery, the moments when we skinny-dipped in the
pond behind the old courthouse after work, ice-skated on the
dark pond lit only by the frozen stars and a waning moon,
walked serenely beneath the elms that didn't even know they
were dying of a strange disease, just as we were not aware of
our lives dying of the strangeness that was creeping between us,
to be parted cruelly and sent away to "repent" (as your mother
called it) and to know the "evil of our ways", which only we
knew as the "beauty of our days" (see, it rhymes) like an old
country song about "parting" and "lonely nights" and all that
sad stuff, except only we remember how we managed the late
night calls when only the trembling wires across the country
kept us connected, when I lay in my bed remembering you and
the telephone would ring and I would know it was you before I
even heard your voice, and now all those years, decades,
lifetimes later, I still know who calls me late at night when
everyone else is sleeping, and asks, "How are you? Really?" and

I tease back with "Who is calling?" and we smile and remember... every moment of those years, decades, lifetimes... every single moment, still alive as long as that telephone continues to ring when you call me in the middle of the night... when you can... (401)

# Black Umbrellas
## by Jared Amos

*T*HE SCHOOL BUS STOPPED TO PICK UP FOUR STUDENTS each weekday in front of the house of the woman they called The Umbrella Lady because she was kind enough to bring out two very pretty umbrellas each morning when rain poured onto the shivering youngsters who were so thankful for the kindness that they left the umbrellas under the nearby pine tree where the woman could retrieve them and passers-by would not notice them, those two beautifully decorated umbrellas, one a copy of a Monet rain scene and the other aflutter with colorful butterflies, so different from the umbrella that the Umbrella Lady must have grown up with, for she was very old, back in a time when she had to carry a black umbrella to school where she was teased mercilessly by the other children since she was the only one with that "new-fangled" contraption with its easily broken spokes that gave way to heavy winds that also damaged the black cloth, apparently the only fabric the umbrella makers could find for their new product, those umbrellas that had replaced the fashionable parasols of decades earlier that came in a variety of pastel colored satins and silks in order to protect unfortunate pale ladies from melting under the hot sun, and now were being replaced to protect all humans from suffering some dreadful consequence if they got wet in the spring when the rains came down hard, which actually spurred the founding of the umbrella industry that came up with an idea to save humanity with black umbrellas, seen bumping together along busy rained-on streets, parked regally in umbrella containers in offices, and spread out in home kitchens, carefully shaken out at the door and closed to protect against the superstitious threat of bad luck if they were to carry an open umbrella inside a building and therefore placed, closed, to drip harmlessly where they resided until the next need for protection against those dreadful, fearsome drops of falling water, the memories of which led the Umbrella Lady to take pity on those unfortunate school children who so resembled her grandchildren, the tykes who were withheld from her by an angry, revengeful son and his wife for some long-forgotten reason, but who haunted the woman daily, wondering where they were and what they were doing and if they even remembered they had a loving grandmother not too far away, longing for them as she gently braved the morning shower to shuffle outside and place her two precious umbrellas under the pine tree for "her children"... (427)

# The Old Woman
## by Emily Jayne Milton

*T*HE OLD WOMAN WEARING A PINK FLANNEL NIGHTGOWN that peeked out from under a tattered gray chenille robe, and an incongruous purple baseball cap, which she wears to hide her thinning hair, doesn't notice her skin has turned to masses of wrinkles and scars and dark blotches because her wandering mind is viewing a picture-show in her head that recalls childhood days soaring on the rope and wood swing her daddy hung in the apple tree for her and her sister (who has long gone to her reward after a lifetime spent seeking forgiveness for her sins), as she remembers the boys who filled the young girl's head with a sense of warm hands, broken promises, flowers and prom night, when she danced — yes, actually danced with her father on prom night — along with memories of her first job as a clerk in a feed store, and her dream job as a journalist which led to meeting two U.S. Presidents, experiencing the wonder of a typhoon, along with memories of the soulful love she found just as predicted in the song about the handsome new man she had "yet to meet walking down a strange new street", who taught her the meaning of love as no one else would teach her, and the pain of losing him that lasted until she was wafted into another romance with another handsome young man who offered her a life of gold and honey, but who turned her life into pain and struggle, receiving two lovely daughters as the only blessings from her marriage, one an energetic, loyal martyr and the other a bitchy, independent belle, with whom she found adventure and promise in starting life anew when she discovered her passion and pursued it through a career that took her on jaunts to Baghdad where she came in contact with her heritage, to Greece where she learned about her natural strength as a woman, to Ireland where she found long lost cousins who tried to talk her into moving them back to America with her, to Spain where she found use for her high school Spanish, and to London where she had tea with the queen, and finally on that long hot cruise through the Caribbean that almost became a catastrophe when the ship was boarded by pirates, all adventures that enriched a life that was nearing its end as she rocked gently on the porch of the Old Folks Home waiting for supper, reviewing once again a long life well lived, and smiling at the beauty of it all... (429)

# Make Your Pet a Celebrity!
## by Sara Jacobelli

S O I GOT LAID OFF FROM THE CHEMICAL PLANT and the ole lady's job slinging hash at the grade school cafeteria pays minimum wage, and unemployment don't pay zilch in Louisiana, plus it'll run out in a few months, and I'm cruising Craigs List, baby, looking for a gig, playing around on the Internet, when I spot this article, "20 Pets Who Made Their Pet Parents Millions on Instagram and YouTube", so that got me thinking, we got a fat black and white cat Zelda who don't do much but lay around and look cute and eat a lot of Friskies and Party Treats, so maybe we could make Zelda an Internet Star, make a lot of money while we're at it, but I'm scrolling through looking at all the other Money-Making Pets and it's hard to compete with skirt-wearing pigs and a naked parrot with no feathers and a dog that looks like a teddy bear and cocktail-sipping squirrels, so I look at Zelda and think, if I could just teach her to talk, I'll post a video of "My Talking Cat Zelda" and then I'll sell tons of advertising for cat food and cat treats and cat litter, so now I gotta plan and I ain't gonna look for another gig, just gonna stay home and teach Zelda the Talking Cat how to talk and maybe even go further than Instagram and YouTube — I'm talking a Web Series here, a weekly show — maybe it'll even get picked up by Amazon or Netflix or HBO, so now me and my ole lady we're on our way from the Poor House to the Rich House and we'll be riding the Gravy Train to Easy Street soon's as I can get the cat to start talking, figuring we'll start with small baby steps, first words, then sentences, you know, and in the meantime I gotta borrow money from my brother-in-law Larry to pay the rent and keep the Internet on, just gotta get Zelda over her shyness and… oh she said her first word just now that was either "no" or "leave me alone" or "that's enough", so before you know it, me and the ole lady's gonna be riding around with a Famous Cat in a brand new Cadillac or Lincoln Continental because I know this is gonna pay off way better than buying lottery tickets or selling weed or hustling shady doctors for pain pills to sell on the street, so wish me luck, we're desperate over here… oh the cat said another word… I think she said, "Stop." (430)

# Motivation
## by Kiki Dayton

*I* WOKE UP THIS MORNING AWARE OF ALL THE VOICES in my head telling me what to eat, what to wear, what to worry about, what's wrong with my life, including voices of my mother, my dad, my nasty sister, my vindictive children, and all the other noxious people in my life: current "friend" who demeans everything I do or say, the client I took to lunch who cattily noticed aloud that I used too much butter on my roll, and goes all the way back to that obnoxious (interesting adjective, so like "noxious" but more-so) college professor who accused me of cheating on a test because I did so well, and, as I lay there remembering all the slights and digs, it became clear why I was so fearful of risking, which made me sit up and face the sun shining in my bedroom window as I vowed to turn off those voices, yes, you heard me, turn them off and begin listening to other voices that tell me how wonderful I am, how I care for wee animals and little children, how I visit old people in their loneliness, and contribute to organizations that aid those less fortunate, and how I have a creative mind that expresses itself through music and art and, of course writing, which is the joy of my life because writing gives me a sense of leaving behind a legacy, if you wish to call it that, for the future through my words that will echo throughout the rest of life on this planet, for everyone knows that books are eternal, whether they are on a computer or in a bookstore or library where others can pick them up and remember that someone with a good mind and willing heart wants… no, cross that out, that someone *needs*… to express themselves for posterity, and they will know that whoever and whatever denigrates and demeans us by getting into our heads can be banished with only the next thought of a beautiful river glittering in the sunlight or a sweet child smiling up at you through tears or the blackness of a starlit sky alive with aurora borealis while motoring across North Dakota, or, trust me, your mother's glorious eyes telling you that what you did wasn't as bad as you think, thus cleansing that precious mind of the negative clutter and replacing it with positive parts of life — hope, trust, reason, responsibility, confidence, love, and wonder, all realizations that perked me up and pushed me out of bed to face another day at the office… (432)

# Deceit
## by Dan Mills

*J*ILLIAN'S SLIPPERS WHISPERED ON THE CRUSHED VELVET carpet as she entered the dimly lit room and cautiously approached a heavy wooden door with cast iron trappings, where she angled her long pointed ears forward and detected low rumbling voices coming from the room next door, but she couldn't hear what they were saying, so Jillian bit her bottom lip and extended the index finger on her left hand toward the large iron doorknob as a static spark shot from the iron fixture which conjured a mental picture of the occupants in the next room, a gray-skinned ogre with protruding lower tusks and a furrowed brow who was towering over two identical halfling brothers with neatly trimmed black beards and an ancient wizard dressed in a tall pointed hat and long flowing robes, who told them that the King was unaware of the situation and wondered if the Queen could hold her tongue and not spoil their plans, just as the wizard shushed them and pointed his gnarled finger toward the door and said that someone was listening to their conversation, a sprite, and Jillian's eyes widened when she drew in a sharp breath just as the wizard cast a spell, turning the doorknob into a serpent that struck at Jillian's hand, which she avoided by pulling away just in time, and her translucent wings became a blur as she flew across the room, leaving a trail of pixie dust floating in her wake as the ogre, wizard, and pair of halflings crashed through the heavy door and followed the glittering trail to the place it disappeared into the nearby woods, where the wizard became furious, telling his followers that if the sprite got away and told the King of their plans, they would surely hang from the gallows, something they all wished to avoid, but the sprite seemed to have vanished into thin air, although Jillian was actually very close by, hugging the far side of a tall spruce tree, her tiny heart beating fiercely in her chest and the side of her face pressed firmly against the trunk of the tree as she held her breath and concentrated on nothing but the cool scent of spruce needles, the stickiness of spruce sap and the roughness of the spruce bark, desperately trying to become part of the wonderful spruce tree, and as soon as the wizard, ogre, and halflings were gone, Jillian could inhale deeply, allow the fresh mountain air to fill her lungs, to re-start her heart and awaken her brain, and then she would warn the King of the deceit that awaited him… (435)

# Closing the Red Door
## by Donna Anderson

W HILE I WALKED DOWN THE STEPS I KNEW I would never come back or ever see again this red door that opened into this house that was supposed to be full of loving people but was actually full of a mother and father who are so judgmental they cannot see I am far more happy living in the compound on Front Street than living here where they constantly point out that I have no money to buy new clothes, nor a place to shower at will, nor a warm and dry place to sleep, but what they don't know, and I'm not telling them, is that I am perfectly happy in my chosen place that overlooks the Puget Sound, that lets me see the seagulls swooping and scoring food, and the sun sparkling on the waves when the wind comes up, and the moon at night with all the stars sending off specks of light to make a fairyland type of setting for all to see on those evenings when the clouds aren't covering them, but when they are, seeing the different layers of gray and white and all the shades in between that proves to me life is ever-changing and I must change with it and not go back to that lousy situation where I am wrong just because I don't want to go into Father's business, and I am wrong just because I don't want to cook with Mother, and just because I love to sing and play my guitar and sit for long hours dreaming and writing songs, I am never going to account for anything like my brother did when he went to college forever to become a doctor, or like my sister did when she married that very rich man and never mind she isn't happy — she is rich and she'll learn to be happy, and they didn't ask me if I had any prospects, but if they had I could tell them about the song I sold and how I now have a contract to write music and songs for a movie production company, and I'm moving to New York and I will travel with the show, and my contract specifies I will be the lead lyric writer for the next five years, and my trip to see them today was to tell them that, but I never got to speak or even to voice an opinion because they know everything and what I want to say doesn't matter, except I know it does matter to me and I'm very, very happy to be away from the negativity and know that now I'm associated with happy positive people and will be for a long time… (453)

# E.C.U.
## by Dan Mills

Gil Tallboy, an officer in the Extraterrestrial Crimes Unit, shifted his supercharged Camaro into fourth gear and stomped down on the accelerator, causing the back tires to chirp, pushing the speedometer past the one-hundred-thirteen miles-per-hour mark and closing the gap between himself and the Scav, a regenerative alien from Proxima B, who glanced into the mirror mounted on the handlebars of the Harley Davidson motorcycle he'd stolen and saw the letters E.C.U., which were printed backwards on the windshield of Gil's Camaro, causing the alien to open up the throttle and lean forward to become more aerodynamic in an attempt to outrun the lawman, but then he turned and fired a weapon at the Camaro, exploding the windshield inward, causing Gil to duck below the dashboard to avoid bits of safety glass that peppered the inside of the car, just before Gil felt the Camaro collide with the motorcycle, causing it to cartwheel into a drainage ditch and launch the Scav through the air and onto the asphalt, while the police car spun donuts down the highway, tires squealing and smoke bellowing from the wheel wells until it finally came to a screeching halt sideways in the road, where Gil switched off the engine, looked out both side windows to make sure no one else was coming down the road, then noticed the Harley Davidson in the ditch with its front forks bent under and the handlebars twisted out of shape, and the alien outlaw lying face down on the highway in an expanding pool of blood, but since this alien was a regenerator and most likely would survive the crash, Gil pulled the sawed-off hack gun from a holster strapped to the driver's seat of the Camaro and jacked a round into the chamber before twisting a dial on the magazine to PUREE as he walked over to the Scav to read him his rights, but before Gil could mirandize the alien, the creature sat up and cackled like a hyena before sliding his prehensile tongue out of his mouth, coiled like a wet, sticky snake ready to strike, a clear warning that Gil was all too familiar with, so when the alien squealed and lunged at him, Gil's hack gun barked and vaporized the Scav's head, but it had little effect on the regenerative alien as he stood up and staggered blindly down the road, at which time Gil levered another round into the hack gun, adjusted the dial to CHUNKY and pulled the trigger again, which sent a load of razor sharp fragments through the alien's upper torso, leaving only his lower extremities kicking and wriggling on the surface of the highway until Gil gathered up the legs and threw them into the trunk of his Camaro, and then headed for the Enid, Oklahoma lockdown so the Scav could regenerate and serve out the rest of his sentence... (484)

# A Sentence Is...
## by Val Dumond

*T*O: MY DEAR WRITER FRIEND JOSEF, who wrote asking what this one-sentence story is all about since Josef has been told and he believed that sentences should be short and never run-on, as you will find this sentence to be, which is why I am writing to tell you that a sentence may take many forms, and over the centuries of English usage, it has done exactly that, running mostly into four types: *simple, compound, complex,* and *compound-complex,* and now there is another, a fifth, that teachers pooh-pooh as "those terrible run-on sentences", but which are coming into their own with a book soon to be published (actually, this one) that is full of sentences written by writers, like you, that run on from 100 to 2000 words and cross all lines that include fiction stories, assessments of technical grammar, business opportunities, and personal memories, but more about that later because at this time I want to describe those standard types of sentences, the four about which I spoke a few lines earlier, beginning with the *simple sentence* that contains only a subject and predicate, or as some have noticed, a noun and verb, but can also include simple modifiers, such as adjectives and adverbs, and phrases (you remember prepositional phrases), and is sometimes referred to as an "independent clause", and the second is the *compound sentence* which is nothing but two or more independent clauses, or in other words, two or more sentences kept together by a semi-colon, comma, or a connecting word, which is to say grammatically, a conjunction, but that is only part of sentence structure, as you will see when we come to the third type of sentence, the *complex sentence* that is composed of both-of-the-above and adds a clause or two, and you will recall that clauses are super-phrases that must include a verb to enjoy the upgrade to clause, and finally, the fourth which is a *compound-complex*

*sentence* and… duh… includes compound sentences with phrases that make it also complex, and now, as if that weren't enough to keep writers' heads spinning for hours, we introduce a fifth kind of sentence, *the one-sentence story*, a sample of which you are reading here that can be as long as you want it, Josef, extending into infinity if you have the patience to stick around that long, but if you don't, you can end it at any time, as if you'd want to unless you're planning to take up the challenge of the one-sentence story and make it as long as you think you can carry on a reasonable story or description, and since I have thoroughly outlined the structure of sentences and, Josef, I believe, answered your doubt about writing a one-sentence story, there isn't much more to say except that I feel so relaxed and ready to go back to work that I'm not sure I can quit this sentence, which means I could keep this going as long as…
(497)

# The Handsome Man
## by Debbie Davidson

*L*EONA, A TALL SLENDER WOMAN IN HER LATE FIFTIES, liked wearing her long curly black hair twisted into a bun in the back while her curls in front were kinked to give height and style, and swooped to one side, fashioned after a look she had seen Lena… hmm, she couldn't recall her last name, however, she was a singer, and many years ago when Leona envisioned herself as beautiful and sophisticated as Lena whatever-her-last-name-is who played in that movie with, was it Cole Porter or that Harry Bella-something, but thought she would never be as rich or renowned as her, yet, she could sit upright and seemingly dignified as she pictured Lena would sit in a doctor's examining room where the décor made it appear to be an examining room with its elevated exam table, an incandescent exam lamp shining down on the empty table and, to her right aligned against the walls five modular base cabinets, one containing a sink, then along the left wall right below the two trio lights, was an instrument panel for the blood pressure sleeve, thermometer, and a medical device she didn't know, but what was happening around her as nurses took her temperature, poked her to locate a blood vessel large enough to draw blood (hers always floated), blurred as she wondered whether the doctor's Alzheimer diagnosis was the reason she couldn't even remember the first name of the handsome older man sitting next to her, but she did recall one time in her life having loved him more than chocolate chip cookies, Butter Pecan ice cream, BBQ ribs, fried catfish, and homemade biscuits… and that is when she stopped wondering about him since her thoughts were not coming together and she couldn't connect one to the other without getting lost into another intriguing thought and toying with it, thinking that maybe his name was Apple Pie, and realizing that seemed silly, so she laughed out loud and the handsome man looked at her, annoyed as if she had done something naughty, so she thought about something really naughty, like kissing him, and that made her laugh harder than before, so she laughed uncontrollably, envisioning herself rolling across the floor while kissing the handsome man until she grew sad thinking he might reject her, but she still felt so tenderly toward him he had to be her older brother, but she thought he had died, as well as she could remember, however, she knew it had been a long time since she last saw her brother, and that is when the handsome man stood up and she felt frightened, but she couldn't figure out why, and that made her even more afraid as the man in the white lab coat took her by the hand, led her to a wheelchair, made her sit down, and then whisked her past the handsome man and she saw him watching her as she turned to glance at his handsome face one more time, but he held his head down in the shame he felt for no longer having the ability, energy, or patience to care for the wife he loved... (525)

# Missing Car Dreams
## by Todd Thompson

*I*F YOU'VE EVER HAD THAT CRAZY DREAM where you can't find your car, remember where it was parked, or even recall why you left it, there is an answer and I can tell you, because I've had that dream — often — and I figured it out, which is what I'm about to tell you, so sit down and prepare yourself to be excited, because the answer is both simple and complicated, so I'm offering the simple answer first, and that is that you don't know either who you are or where you are going, hence the reference to the car because all guys know that the car you drive represents who you are, what you like (and can afford) and what makes you enjoy your travels, as well as where you are in life, just around the corner, hidden in somebody's garage, or parked on some side street waiting to find the main avenue to success, which is what most of us are looking for, but the more complicated version has to do with who you want to accompany you on your travels, as if you get to choose rather than take who your choices may be, such as family who we don't always get to choose, or friends who somehow are put in our paths, some forced upon us, and some just out of our reach, as if you don't recall that lone dream where you couldn't find your car, but you knew where it was and you just couldn't find the right streets or paths to get to it, which makes for intense feelings of futility when you wake up, as do most of the dreams about missing cars — giving you those extraordinary feelings when you wake up — but we're not there yet in our explanations, just approaching the more complex nature of the choices of who you want to accompany you in your travels, loved ones or those characters you encounter who offer an enormous variety of silly or serious challenges, the people who make life interesting thus worth living, and if you choose "loved ones", you've taken the easy road, but if you choose "characters with challenges", you've shown yourself to be of a nature that invites variety, invites the unusual, invites the major interests of life, and which writers seek most diligently when writing their stories, because the "easy" choices don't make for much action or fun either, unless they include criminals, police, or one of those clowns who jazz up parties, but if you choose the honest-to-god challenging messed-up characters, you have something to work with, such as obstacles to overcome, problems to solve, troubles to work your way out of (can't stop here because that would be ending a sentence with a preposition, wouldn't it), so you can bet I'll summarize the real meaning of the missing car dreams as the search for that which makes you whole, that which makes you happy, and that which satisfies a deep craving, the eternal itch, the infinite yearning to know all there is to know about your world, but more importantly, all there is to know about you and where you're headed, which is always elusive because... (535)

# Baggage
## by Nick Romeo

P LEASE TRUST ME, BECAUSE THIS MAY SOUND CRAZY, but it all started when the coach disputed the ref's call by kicking him in the shins, so the ref threw another penalty flag then ran to the center of the field, blew his whistle, waved his arms around as if he was swatting flies, and announced to the crowd, "unsportsmanlike conduct", adding "the coach will serve the penalty by sitting on the opposing team's bench so that the fans can throw bottled water, beer, rocks, or anything they want at him," after which various members of the coach's team decided to get revenge after hearing that call, well, actually the whole team went berserk, at least everyone except for the towel boy and cheerleaders since the towel boy hung himself off the goal post after the first quarter, and the cheerleaders were too busy sharing needles to notice anything on the field, *trust me*, I'm not even at the worst part yet and we have to leave the house soon, but as I was saying, the team with the knee-jerk coach beat the opposing team's kicker with baseball bats until he stopped squirming, and this caused that *same* team to get another "unsportsmanlike conduct" penalty which got the entire team ejected, so the cheerleaders had to sub, but who says women can't play a man's game, or drugs are bad for the body, because they ran a Triple-Reverse Statue of Liberty Flea Flicker and got a 95-yard touchdown in their first play, but the ref threw another penalty flag with the announcement of an "ineligible receiver down field", causing the quarterback cheerleader to kick the ref in the groin, which made the ref throw another penalty flag, with *another* announcement (slightly higher pitched) to the crowd of "unsportsman... er... unsportspersonlike conduct", while at that same moment several cheerleaders created a distraction by mud wrestling around center field, while the team's coach, who was still confined to the opposing team's bench covered with popcorn and soda, used this eye-candy diversion to challenge the play by tying the red challenge flag to a lawn dart, rubbing a poison frog on the tip, and throwing it high into the air where it eventually landed in the ref's shoulder, knocking him out immediately, when the defending team decided to dump Gatorade on the ref, but he did not stir while they went through his pockets, removed his shoes, and ran off the field to the parking lot just as the spectators started brawling in the stands, which I watched as people got hit and dropped all around me, and it was then a yellowish-orange portal opened in the sky, a giant ship emerged, and a multitude of mini-rocket-propelled pods steered by green aliens with giant eyes flew out of the spaceship and attacked the crowd, launching photon beams and giant nets to capture whatever survivors they could... so anyway because we don't have much time, let's grab our Bugout-Bags and run to a safe place *not too far* from here that I've been preparing in case this would happen, and please quit shaking your head because, *trust me*, I've never lied to you — well, maybe once or twice, but not this time — and please don't look outside until we're ready to go... at which time...

she looks outside
    and turns pale... (561)

# The Strange Death
# at Poinciana House
## by Angela Vonmizener

A UGUSTUS OOLY NAMYSH STARED OUT the huge window of his beloved home, which he had named Poinciana House, quite possibly because this Caribbean dream home of his was surrounded entirely by Poinciana trees, whose brilliant orangey-red blossoms extended on either side of them like so many wild and undisciplined umbrellas, blowing around like dancers in the Caribbean breezes, and he wondered vaguely whether he had done the right thing inviting three more-or-less complete strangers into his home on some sort of wild spurt of generosity or possibly merely a capricious whim that he was starting to question now, as he realized that his English side was the more expansive, and his Russian side far more cautious, secretive, guarded, and less given to spurts of unpredictability, except that he had noticed that in his sculptures, he did seem to have found that artistic freedom and wildness when creating one of his famous *heads*, for which he charged some wealthy soul several thousands of dollars, one of which personages was due to arrive momentarily by helicopter, since his lovely domicile, perched on a high hill overlooking the turquoise and royal blue waters that surround Marabunta Island, can only be reached by donkey or helicopter, with two of her friends, who had agreed to accompany her, and had been invited by Mr. Namysh as his guests, in spite of the fact that he was not personally acquainted with them, although he had heard of the diplomat, Sir Victor Hazlitt, but had no ken of the other gentleman who was by way of being, apparently, an actor of some considerable talent and who quite possibly might even have the funds to purchase an original Namysh work of art, and Augustus, known as *Gus* to intimate friends, had just the piece that this actor might enjoy, one he had named the "Head of the Gorgon", or quite possibly it might appeal to the lady in question, namely Lady Augusta Armstrong, who had a great weakness for celebrities and for famous pieces of art, in which she greedily immersed herself, and perhaps she would be the one to buy the Gorgon's head, a possibility that seemed more likely to Mr. Namysh who tapped his small pudgy fingers together with enthusiasm while he pondered this plausible possibility, for after all, it was not for nothing that this rotund, portly little man had been referred to by the intelligentsia and those in the know as the world's most celebrated and sought-after sculptor who had closeted himself away on a tiny island, preferring solitude and isolation to a gregarious life in London or a hectic social whirl of a life in New York, where he could not have embraced his Muse to the level that he could at his island house, where he could invite certain people to come and visit him on his own terms, and Lady Armstrong, whom he had met on many occasions, certainly was a lady whose mind and brain he had admired greatly, to the extent that he felt she could help him with a problem that he had, and possibly her two companions might also be able to put in their "two cents worth", but that remained to be seen, he thought, for this problem was one that he could not fight alone, and involved the very life of one that he held most dear... (563)

# A Stranger in the Village
## by Angela Richardson

*I* FIND MYSELF STANDING IN THE MIDDLE OF THE ROAD in a tiny village not far from the Sea and notice that all the villagers have retired to the coolness of their stone houses, seeking what relative shelter there may be from a merciless heat, and the only living things I see around me are a camel who appears tall and elegant, seemingly impervious to the suffocating heat of the day, tethered outside one of the curious flat-roofed houses as it watches all about him with an aristocratic eye, and a small donkey, grey-eared with soft eyes, seeking some respite beneath the date palm, its head hung low, motionless, and as I watch this, I am surprised to see a figure walking towards me, slowly, but with measured pace and purpose, and although I cannot see this man, for it is indeed a man, I am filled with a strange feeling that I cannot for the life of me put well into words, for the words seem strange within my head, odd and inadequate, because I am a little frightened and I am quite excited, but I am at peace, and I am moved, and as I see the figure get a little closer, I tremble, for I know who He is, and He, astonishingly, knows who I am, yet approaches closer and closer, and I cannot run, for my feet are rooted to the ground, and He seems to move in a little cloud of dust that puffs up into the heated air as He gets closer and closer, and in an instinctive movement, I fall to my knees on the ground and feel the hot dry dust touch my hair, and hope that perhaps He will pass me by, but He does not, and I am suddenly aware that He stands in front of me, for as I open my eyes very cautiously I see two feet before me, shod in well-worn, faded leather sandals that have been stitched and re-stitched, and I see that the feet are covered with a soft dry desert dust, and without knowing why, I gently touch the tired feet, and remove what dust from them that I can by passing my fingers across them, and to my astounded ears I hear Him say, in an oh-so-gentle voice, "Look at me," and I am too moved to speak until He speaks again, "Look at me, little one," and obediently I raise my head and look into the most beautiful face that I have ever seen, for it is a tanned face, a strong face, of such noble expression that I know I am looking at the King, and then I feel the touch of His hand, extraordinarily strong yet gentle, and then from somewhere, from Heaven perhaps, I have the courage to speak, and I ask, "Sir, what would you have me do?" and he answers softly, "Go and be kind... to all... to everyone, without exception, that is what I would have you do, now go in peace, my daughter," and with these last words, He moves away from me, slowly disappearing into the hot dusty mist of the day, while I feel my eyes wet with tears that sting my face with their saltiness, as I realize that God has reached out His Hand and given me my life's lesson, for now my life can never be the same again, and I find myself wondering whether He has ever done this before to the least of His, like me... (589)

# Death Comes Calling
## by Diane H. Larson

*H*E DID NOT HEAR OR SEE HER COME IN, which in itself was unusual as he made it a point to be attentive to those who entered his establishment, and this was the reason he had hung the bell on the door… to help him spot the troublemakers so that he could keep an eye on them… for with a lifetime of experience behind him, he knew who they were as soon as he saw them, and since there was no one else in the bar, he should have noticed her, so maybe he really was losing his edge, and for the umpteenth time the idea of retirement slipped into his mind and then just as quickly slid out because he knew he would never retire, for this was where he belonged, and more than likely, he would die here, but a nagging feeling in his gut had drawn his eyes to the corner table by the window where she sat in the shadows, her fingers drumming on the scarred tabletop, no doubt tapping along to some fast-paced rhythm in her head, those fingers on hands that had seen more years of hard work than his own well-worn paws, and he was no spring chicken, and although her face was turned toward the window so he could not see her expression, he knew that she was traveling down some distant pathway in her mind, as he did plenty of that… sometimes with pleasure, sometimes with regret… more often than not these days with such an overwhelming guilt that he was soon sent rushing back to reality, so perhaps he had simply been wandering down one such pathway when she came in, which might explain why he had missed her, for these days it seemed that the past was more alive than the present for him, but he could sense the tension in her body, as if she was waiting for someone… a long lost lover perhaps, a child she had abandoned, an old friend she had not seen in years, or maybe she was waiting to forgive someone… or would she be like him, the one needing to ask for forgiveness, and would that be as hard for her as it had always been for him, or could she be carrying some deep dark secret that she wanted to share before she died, or perhaps she was just killing time as he was, waiting for the inevitable to come along and, as he wondered about these things, he started toward the table to take her order because, after all, that was his job, but for some reason he hesitated, feeling strangely shy, as if he were once again a small schoolboy approaching an overpowering presence, though why he felt this way he had no idea since he was not afraid of anyone or anything anymore, yet in that moment he felt more afraid than he had ever felt in his life, and he was tempted to turn and flee, but this was his place, his duty, so he kept moving, and when he approached her, he slurred his words to cover the quiver in his voice when he asked her what he could get for her, and very slowly, she turned her head and focused her gaze fully on him, and when he looked into her fiery eyes, he knew immediately who she was and why she had come, and he no longer felt afraid as she murmured, "Red wine please, just a small glass for I won't be here long." (591)

# Blue Tarp Mania
## by Ruth Anderson

*T*HEY SUDDENLY POPPED UP ALL OVER THE NORTHWEST landscape, large blue tarps covering firewood, plants, cars, bikes, and people, all made of some kind of organic cloth from China, which gave me and Joe the idea to grow the plant that they used to manufacture the material, and so we bought a few acres out in the country by a lake and imported these spindly plants that eventually bloomed with bright blue blossoms like the blue bonnet on the margarine package, and we harvested them at just the right time and sold them to a tent plant, and then folks started asking us where we got the plants, so we started propagating them in friends' yards, empty fields, and all over the place because they were popular and looked beautiful when they bloomed in July, and pretty soon if you flew over Pierce County, Washington, you'd see fields of these delightful blue plants that were quickly turned into blue tarps, and those tarps proliferated because people bought them to create little houses that were badly needed because the area had a lot of homeless folks, and me and Joe ended up getting an award from the governor for solving the housing shortage, which we were mighty honored to receive, and then we realized the tents might be even more suited to California, so we drove to Los Angeles to market the tents because it never rains in the desert and wouldn't those bright blue plants and tarps and tents look good in the desert, but we needed to find a T-shirt company to produce some bright blue shirts we could use for marketing, until Joe said we shouldn't get in over our heads because who knew if blue tents would be as fascinating for desert folks as they were for Northwest folks who love anything that isn't green on account of having all the green, and at that point we decided to turn around and go back home because even though the tents had some issues in bad weather, we could maybe add something to the manufacturing that would help stabilize the organic material, but as we were driving up I-5 past Centralia, Washington, on a very windy day, a gust blew the blue tarp off a truck ahead of us and stuck to our windshield, and I had the devil's own trouble to get off the highway so we could remove the tarp and that gave us the idea to market the tarps to the US Army, reckoning soldiers could mount them on the back of trucks in war-torn places and release them when they happened on enemy vehicles, so that those drivers would drive off the road and our soldiers could capture them and their goods, shortening wars by months if not years, all because me and Joe were wise enough to create blue tarps from those spindly plants, and maybe farmers in poor countries could raise the plants, and eventually even in the desert nations and the jungle, so everyone would be sheltered in comfort under the blue tents, and we'd win a Nobel prize for peace because living under a blue tent soothed the soul and made folks more peaceful, and then with the Nobel prize money we could hire some scientists to figure out how the tent material could give off nourishing food, sort of like growing mushrooms inside a dark place, and that food would be like manna, and then the Pope would reward us for taking care of the lowliest and we could retire, knowing we had saved humankind — all because of the Northwest and its love affair with blue tarps! (608)

# How Can You Call It Love When...
## by Bill Kaiser

*H*OW CAN YOU CALL IT LOVE WHEN THE HEART IS MISSING? sounds like a good old country wailing song similar to the ones that begin with "I woke up this morning..." which is the way most of us start our days, but these words reflect the feelings of many of us who looked for love and grabbed the first thing that came along, whether or not it was real love or not, but we called it that anyway, as if we wanted to define love as an attraction, which it definitely is, but how that attraction shows up is entirely another story because most times sex rears its head and we "fall" for it, expecting sexual compatibility to carry us through all the years of togetherness, whether or not it is a marriage or a partnership or a relationship, and how soon we figure out that sexual attraction fades as the years pass, with the possible exception of those who have unfathomable sexual appetites, and we come to know that keeping up an attraction through appetite takes work, which most of us don't have time for in the middle of holding down a job, working to pay the mortgage, paying for the kids' clothes and such, maintaining friendships and interests of the kind that keep the individual whole, and recognizing the need for companionship which, if the heart is missing from this endeavor (if we can call a relationship an "endeavor") there is little reason to continue, which is the sad part of my country wailing song, for the words continue in this way: *"How can you call it love when the heart is missing, when we end the kissing, when we start the hissing, how can you call it love, for only the heart knows what it wants, what it needs to be whole, and only the real thing can make up the soul, so when you find love, check it out at the start and know that there ain't much love without a true heart,"* and that's the way real love shows up to those who are lucky enough to find it, which usually means you have to look for it, search high and low everywhere, keep your senses alert, and when you think you've found love, give it the old country song test, asking, *"How can you call it love when the heart is missing?"* as if your life depends on it, which it does because love without heart is not love but a poor joke played on the unwary who don't give a whit about anyone but themselves and their selfish needs and who don't deserve love because they have no heart to begin with, which begs the question, how can you call it love when you are heart-less, incapable of love because to really be in love takes a heart, and anyone who thinks they can fake love by using other means is only kidding themselves in ways that is unhealthy for them as well as unfair to their partner, especially if a marriage and children are involved, because what happens is the tragedy of a wife's infidelity and pain to the husband, as well as insecurity and doubt among the children, so my plea is to be patient and wait for the right heart to come along, at which time you will recognize that it must be shared and that you have the right heart to share back… believe me, I know…and you will emerge from this vale of tears and pain into a valley of sunshine and happiness beyond anything you have ever experienced because that is what it means to share your heart, that is what is called Love with a capital L…. (610)

# All the Way from Tacoma to Tucson
## by Annette Munoz

S ARA JANE SLAMMED SHUT THE HATCH on her 17-year-old
white Eclipse after filling every bit of available space with
packing boxes of all shapes and sizes, including a box of
hardcover books, three boxes of clipped recipes (Sara Jane
loved to cook), sentimental items like the small ceramic
bluebird she'd won in 1960 at the Puyallup Fair, and the small,
gold-edged shoji screen she'd bought on her trip to Japan in
1998, along with unboxed things like the big heavy hammer
(carefully tucked under the driver seat, next to her 46-year-old
rolling pin) that had belonged to her late first husband in the
1970s when he was still a journey carpenter, plus two shoe
boxes filled with music CDs ranging from the full Beatles
collection to her opera collection with picks like "Madame
Butterfly" (which always made her think of the time in the late
1990s when she and a friend went to see that opera in Seattle,
and during intermission when they went to the lobby to buy a
glass of champagne there was a 5.0 earthquake which, at first
they both thought was a truck hitting the building, and then,
when they realized it was an earthquake, they were so glad it
was during intermission and not during that beautiful aria
while they were sitting up in the high balcony in the cheap
seats) and "La Boheme" (she loved romantic opera, especially
by Puccini, but also dark works like "The Ring"), to some of her
favorite musicals like "Les Miserables" and "Phantom of the
Opera", and old rock and roll CDs, along with a couple CDs
she'd picked up especially for this long, long drive — country
music, which seemed to make sense for a drive to Tucson —
including the new Keith Urban album and an older one by
Darius Rucker, and at the last minute she'd included the old
Three Tenors CD that her second late husband played (in

cassette form) in his white Mercedes coupe, way back in 1992 during that fateful drive in an early December snowstorm from Brugge to Antwerp when she realized she was falling in love with that Dutchman — oh, but darn it, that was long, long before he became alcoholic and all they did was fight and then ultimately he died and now she had sold the house in which she had tried so hard to make a home for twenty-nine years, the home where she raised her now estranged daughter, she thought wistfully, as she finally bent down and snuggled her little dog into his small space carved out with blankets in the back seat behind the front passenger seat, surrounded by boxes of clothes (since the front seat was piled with two suitcases stacked one on top of the other, and the floor space in front held her camera gear and a big bag of snacks) and Sara Jane finally climbed in behind the wheel, put the car in gear, and backed out of the garage for the last time, down the driveway for the last time, up the street to the arterial that would lead her to I-5 in Tacoma where she had lived for all of her 66 years, and down the 1,600 miles south to her new Tucson home, to the small two-bedroom, two-bath stucco with a red tile roof and a little wash beyond the backyard where already she had seen coyotes and mule deer and javelinas, exactly the kind of house she had always dreamed of owning, the home where she would make new memories surrounded by mountains and Saguaro cactus and mesquite trees, while learning to open her heart again, perhaps even to love again, to live happily ever after… the end. (622)

# Hard Labor
## by Diane H. Larson

*H*ER GUT ACHED, AND HER THROAT BURNED with regurgitating acid, and she felt utterly miserable, so maybe she shouldn't have stopped taking the damn pills, but she had needed to know if they were causing the itching, and yet it always seemed to be the same old story… damned if you do and damned if you don't… and, as if that weren't enough, she felt depressed, though she supposed that just might have something to do with the no sugar, no chocolate, no alcohol, no fat, and therefore… NO FUN… diet she was trying to convince herself to start, which would be enough to depress anyone, but of course it couldn't have anything at all to do with the writing group that she'd attended that afternoon, even though she wondered why she'd bothered to go in the first place, and why she had ever thought for one moment that she could write a good book, especially after growing up with parents who had brought her up to do as she was told, to be obedient, who never taught her to think for herself or to believe she would amount to very much, always comparing her with her brother who was the "creative one" in the family, since, after all, she was only a girl, and back in those days, girls were just supposed to learn how to cook, keep house, and take care of their families, not that she was ever particularly wonderful at doing any of that, but she did have one acceptable creative gift and that was to give birth, which was fine, as long as the babies came out beautiful and perfect, as nothing less would suffice, and somehow she had managed to do that exceedingly well, though her perfect babies had grown up into all-too-human adults, and there was not a thing she could do about that now, even if she had wanted to, and, as she thought about it, she realized that the book she had written was much like another one of her babies, only this one had incubated for years, not months, the long and painful labor still in process, with no end in sight, and of course, she couldn't push it out into the world until she knew it would be beautiful and perfect, as nothing less would suffice, but the long labor had begun to take its toll on her aging body, for she had learned early on to stuff her feelings into places that were now wearing out from overuse, and she knew that if she kept this up, it would end up killing her, and anyway, if truth be told, she desperately wanted to bring her creative self out into the world, for she believed that she had a great mind and heart with much to say that she so wanted to share, though somehow she felt she could never birth what she held inside her into exactly the right words, so that they would come out the way she wanted… beautiful and perfect… and that made her wonder about maybe giving it all up and just going back to learning to be a better housekeeper, cook, mother, wife, grandmother, all those "womanly things" her parents had wanted for her, but she knew, without a doubt, that doing that meant death for her spirit for sure, and besides, it was far too late now as the egg had been fertilized and the full-grown fetus had entered the birth canal, so she couldn't possibly abort, and yet she couldn't seem to give birth either… and then it hit her with a shock that her book was not all that was stuck in the birth canal… no wonder she felt so miserable! (624)

## MAMA – A Liberated Woman Before Her Time
### by Betty Moorhead

*M*AMA WAS BORN IN 1895 and in her early forties, (the mother of eight) took her first step toward independence when a neighbor gave Mama driving lessons, and one day she came in with the neighbor's car parked at the curb, saying, "Come get in the car, kids, because I'm taking you for a ride" and we three youngest kids, Maxine, Jimmy, and I, ran out the door and piled in the neighbor's car, bug-eyed to watch Mama climbing into the driver's seat, knowing we were ready for the adventure, but with no automatic transmission, just a gear shift on the floor and a clutch, the car lurched ahead and we hopped and jumped around the block, Mama braking to a stop back in front of our house, beaming with pride, but as things turned out that was Mama's last drive because she was forced to accept that Daddy meant it when he asked her why she was learning to drive when she didn't have a car and certainly was NEVER going to drive his, but, undaunted, with only an eighth grade education because when her mother died she had to leave school to care for younger siblings, she proceeded to start looking for a job and never having worked outside the home, she first applied to Fulton Bag Cotton Mill reportedly asking them if they wanted to "hire any hands" and even though the answer was "no", Mama was determined and next applied to Woolworth's in downtown Atlanta where she was hired and began work the next Monday, but was let go on Friday because her cash register was out of balance every day, and on her last day the supervisor watched Mama and figured out that when she rang up a sale, instead of registering the amount of the sale, Mama put in the amount of money she was handed, meaning if Mama sold an item for $1 and the customer handed her a $5 bill, she rang up $5, but even with her record she knew that she'd get a job somewhere because World War II was raging and anyone could get a job — even Mama — so she was soon hired by McCrory's, a small department store where she found her niche and enjoyed a successful eight-year career before moving on to bigger and better positions, and for all the years she worked she carried a shopping bag with her home-cooked lunch, which was always a full course meal in jars, with meat, vegetables, salads, homemade biscuits or cornbread, and dessert which made her become popular quickly with co-workers who enjoyed sharing her lunch and hearing her entertaining stories, as Mama loved to laugh and didn't hesitate to tell embarrassing stories about herself, never pretending to be someone she wasn't, a talent that made friends for her from all walks of life, and in addition she always was available to help a friend in need, and after she finished raising her eight children, she blossomed with an ever-lengthening list of organizations she belonged to, which always gave her things to do and places to go, one of them being at age sixty-seven the oldest participant in a fifteen-mile walk for a cause I can't remember and which put her picture in the local newspaper, as well as traveling with the "Goldie-Oldies" all over the country, staying active in church groups and civic groups, belonging to a "quilting bee" where she made beautiful quilts for her children, always staying the eternal optimist no matter how bad things might have been, because Mama always was determined to find the silver lining while raising her children from the 1920s to the 1950s, through economic depression and war, sickness and death, good times and bad, and she stayed indomitable against all odds, years ahead of the times because Mama was an early "liberated" woman, blooming wherever she was planted... (645)

# Home is in the Heart
## by Betty Moorhead

*T*HE RINGING PHONE WOKE ME WHILE IT WAS STILL DARK outside, suggesting bad news, before I heard Dan say "Maxine's gone," and I wanted to scream but didn't for his sake more than mine, because we're not a family of screamers because I learned that lesson early that as a middle child, the sixth of eight children with three older sisters plus two older brothers, one younger sister, and one younger brother, Jimmy (Mama's last baby, the first of us to join the choir of angels watching over us, as I'd always wanted to believe), I knew my family position was the luckiest because my three older sisters became second mothers to me beginning when I was eight and the first of my many nieces and nephews was born, giving me the opportunity to spend almost every weekend at one or another of my sisters' houses helping with their children, or being paid twenty cents a week to dust Hazel's (my oldest sister) house, a generous rate for an eight- or nine–year-old in the depression years of the 1930s when everyone was poor, but I didn't know it because my father had a secure job as a policeman — detective in the beautiful southern city of Atlanta — so even though we had more children than bedrooms, meaning we always slept two to a bed, sometimes three, we were never hungry, always warm, wore new shoes twice a year as well as two new outfits a year (one for Easter and one when school started), so even though we were not an expressive family, I never heard the words "I love you" until just before I married, and I guess I felt the security of being taken care of, even spoiled in some ways, having strong feelings for all my family, wanting to see them frequently, to be of help when needed even after I left the family nest when I was twenty-one and moved 2,000 miles across the country never to live at home again, but I always knew where "home" was, as strong urges took me back there once a year unless I was living across an ocean, which I was some years, and no matter how old we all got, each of us, including me, with homes and children of our own, in my heart my real "home" was always back in Georgia where my original family lived, with long distance calls being way too expensive to make and scary when you received one because most of the time they only came when there was really bad news to report, we kept in touch with handwritten letters, and after mailing them I watched for the postman eagerly every day hoping for a reply until, in my thirties with my parents in their seventies, I started splurging and calling Mama every week just to make sure she was okay and to hear her voice for a short time, so after she passed away I started calling Hazel weekly for the same reasons I'd called Mama — I still needed my family — and before too long I was calling Evelyn and Lillian weekly also until each of them passed away, with all three of my brothers already gone, leaving only Maxine (my younger sister) and me left, and it never entered my mind that Maxine would die before me because, after all, she was younger than me, but the unimaginable happened when Maxine's life ended, so now I have no one waiting for my weekend call and I can tell you it is a very lonely feeling knowing that my old "home" and loved ones are all gone, and even though I have children and grandchildren who love me and all of whom I love with all my heart, it's totally different from what it was for the little girl with a big family that I used to be and still am — that little girl in my heart... (661 words)

# Let's Talk Bridge...
## by Kelyan Conn

Y EARS AGO MY FATHER GENGA CONN INHERITED a bridge across a New York river and when he died he left it to my mother Betta Conn who loved the bridge and re-named it in honor of her mother Lynnbrook and when my dearly beloved mother died she left it to me and now I have in my possession this beloved bridge which I find has become too much for me to handle (pivot) inasmuch as I a native New Yorker have recently moved to Washington DC to be near my beloved clients who clearly need my services and am unable therefore to care for my bridge (pivot) but listen what people need to understand because common people get confused and that is why I need to absolutely find a way to locate someone who will love this wonderful bridge as much as I and my parents and grandparents have loved it and this is why I am appealing to you to make me an offer to make this bridge your own and take care of it as my family has done for decades (pivot) which is making regular visits to see that it remains strong and serviceable for the many people who depend on it to get to their wonderful jobs every day and to return to their happy homes every evening because sometimes the bridge needs special attention going forward (pivot) such as in the spring when the river overfills with water coming from spring rains and melting snow from the wonderful Appalachians (pivot) where my family always took me and my brothers and sisters every summer for a family vacation and where they would afterwards go back to New York leaving us to attend a summer camp (pivot) that allowed us to make fun of the poor kids who didn't have life as good as we did and listen let's agree that it was fun until they started to call us bullies and ganged up on us and forced my dear parents to come get us and take us home which wasn't our fault and is what we wanted all the time anyway (pivot) and we'd all go back and visit the bridge and inspect it and then return to our gorgeous wonderful home that sat high on a hill so we could overlook all the common people below us and know that we were blessed because we had it so good we could afford to own a real bridge which now (pivot) look the truth is we must turn it over to some lucky new owner who could be you if only you took a few minutes to think about how wonderful you would feel owning a real New York bridge like it would be wonderful real wonderful since this would be number one for you (pivot) like you could cross it without paying those irksome tolls that make so many common people unhappy and you could paint it any color you like although the gold that my father painted it has remained the favorite of the family over the years (pivot) but the time has come oh my to bid the beloved wonderful bridge goodbye and make it yours and yes we can turn it over to you in a New York minute ((pivot) as soon as you pay for it and you know that you can raise the money quickly because we're sure you have stashed away funds in the Caribbean somewhere as we also do and (pivot) you can just write a check today and make this wonderful bridge yours all yours and all you have to do is give me a call at a number to be given you when (pivot) you meet me at the Conn Towers at noon tomorrow with a blank check in hand and don't be late because I am a busy person and cannot sit around in my golden apartment waiting (pivot) to meet the hundreds of people who want to make this wonderful bridge theirs and (pivot... plié... and bow) I guarantee it'll be wonderful... (680)

# Just One Sentence!
## by Betty Moorhead

S OMETHING THAT IS REALLY BOTHERING ME RECENTLY is the fact that writers all around me are cranking out one-sentence stories that go on and on and on and on, one page after another and all fitting together nicely to make a story, yet every time I sit down and try to write just one sentence and have it hang together with a common thread, I am quickly soured on it because I constantly feel the need to stop and breathe or go to the bathroom or get a drink of water or answer one phone call or another and lose track of my thoughts and have a hard time remembering what I was thinking when I began this ridiculous task so that it will at least resemble a story when I finally decide that all good things must come to an end while knowing that hard work is always rewarded if I keep going although I doubt that part about hard work being rewarded as I have known many people who have never worked hard a day in their life and seem to have been rewarded over and over again for which I think was not much of an effort, but then I remember that one time in my life I was rewarded for almost no effort at all, just for identifying twelve pages in Oprah's magazine that featured a Christmas ornament, when she sent me three huge boxes of individually wrapped Christmas presents that included an Apple I-Pod that I never used once, a TV set that is now in my grandsons' playroom, about a dozen bracelets and other pieces of jewelry including a very expensive Tiffany bracelet, a leather quilted biker jacket, silver Reebok sneakers, a Samsung cell phone, a Tiffany heart locket necklace, monogrammed playing cards, blue cotton pajamas supposedly worth almost $200, but I can't imagine anyone ever paying $200 for PJs, as I know I wouldn't and I'm guessing you wouldn't either, an art watch and much more stuff that I never knew I needed and certainly had never wanted, but I do have to admit that the two free trips were fun, especially the one with my only granddaughter, Paige, to Los Angeles to see the Ellen Show when Paige got sick with food poisoning after our breakfast at the hotel not long before we were due to be picked up for our flight home, followed by the trip to Chicago to see The Oprah Show with my daughter, Heidi, where we met up with my sister-in-law, Michelle, and her husband whose name I've forgotten because Michelle left him so many years ago and has since left the husband who came after, because some people's lives make me dizzy and I'm sure glad that my life, hard as it has been at times, wasn't hard for the same reasons that Michelle's was hard and I'll always love her to pieces because since the day Chuck, husband Number Two, introduced me to his sister she has truly been a sister to me and I wish we could see each other more often, but she is now living near her daughter in southern California while I'm being watched over by my family in Washington, and even though I was in California recently I could not reach Michelle, hard as I tried so we could arrange a rendezvous, but I learned after I got home that I was still using her old email address which was going to her last husband who apparently still uses that account and also explains why once in a while I still get something from him that I never read, plus I also had old phone numbers for her all of which I have since corrected but far too late to see her again, so I'm hoping when I go to California early next year I will see her but, anyway, I'm feeling better about everything now since I've talked to Michelle and have proved to myself and a few other writers that I can and did write a one-sentence story... (682)

# Rumba
## by Debbie Davidson

ANITA COULDN'T REMEMBER THE LAST TIME she sat down at her dining room table because there seemed no reason to set the table for one and expend all her energy pondering what to cook for one, so she grabbed a teaspoon out of the kitchen drawer, just one, then replaced it, shutting the drawer with her left hip then, knowing what she would do, unable to exercise self-control anymore, she reopened the drawer and pulled out a tablespoon, sensing it was going to be a rough one and she'd get sick and gain more weight, but she felt compelled to battle the mental anguish she experienced every time she thought about the cute little boys with big brown eyes that used to be such momma boys when they were growing up but now, as grown men with their own families (Rodney and his wife Glenda had two girls and a boy while Zachery and Denise had three boys), plus jobs, sports, dance lessons, swimming lessons and a host of other excuses for not picking up the phone or driving to see their mother who they knew lived alone since their dad passed away over seventeen years ago, so she glanced at her large image in the car window as she passed her SUV to get the gallon of Mocha Almond Fudge ice cream out of the freezer to calm the feeling that was eating at her and to devour it to feel better, but she knew the truth and the truth was she wouldn't feel better and she couldn't fit into most of her clothes anymore and that really bothered her because she used to absolutely love the way she looked in her clothes since she felt she had a sense of style between youth and middle-age which kept her really looking younger than she was, and as she walked out of the garage toward the kitchen she could hear the faint sound of that song she had heard many times before when the boys were growing up but now, however, as "Carol of the Bells" rumbaed through her mind from one side of her brain to the other she remembered Christmas time at the Simmons when the boys on Christmas Eve would beg her, "Mommy please can we open just one present before we go to bed, just one mommy?" and she remembered the goodies she loved baking for them, especially their favorite lemon pie with the Philadelphia Cream Cheese, Kraft Cool Whip and C&H Pure Cane Powdered Sugar filling and a buttery Nabisco Honey Maid Graham cracker crust, to devour Christmas morning after they had raced down the stairs scaring her and Ken almost to death thinking they might fall and mess up Christmas, but they never did, probably because she and Ken prayed each night asking the Lord to protect them, especially on holidays, and she remembered how, when Ken passed away, the laughter and play fighting ceased since they simply didn't want to reminisce about their dad yelling at them to stop fighting and come watch the game with him, which they loved doing, and that really hurt because Anita had no one to talk to about Ken, not anyone who wouldn't judge her harshly for not letting go of his memory since it had been so long, that consequently she not only felt lost and without purpose for the years when the boys began having their own families, but she also felt she lost those years right after Ken passed, however, she wasn't blaming the boys, who loved their dad, and besides, her attitude changed as well, since she just couldn't engage in being happy, and now that tune, "Carol of the Bells", rumbaing through her mind sparked conflicting memories of joy as she shut her eyes and envisioned her baby boys' admiration and love for their mother, and the tears poured uncontrollably down her face, latching onto the crevices of yesteryear and into the bowl of melting ice cream reminding her of the years she lost grieving her sense of who, she wanted to be again: Momma… (684)

# It's in the Bloodline
## by Peggy Rose Webster

R ASTUS, A MEMBER OF THE ROYAL BLOODLINE of the barking shih tzus of Ancient China, stood wearing camouflage attire looking wistfully into the sunset as the truck bounced down the road and out of view to the impending and uncertain drop-off at the invisible area around the corner and up the hill where Jack the rat terrier and Jill the dachshund lay waiting for their saving pickup ride to the land of milk and honey, not knowing that Rastus — golden brown and unusually stout — was watching to alert the guards of this intrusion of foreigners coming into their plentiful land with attitudes of wistful ways that only dogs of a certain type have been privy to, not because they did not understand the emotion, but because they had been retained behind a fence in the castle up on the hill that Rastus guarded and wondered why they had not been let loose to roam the vast estate, and then it was clear that they had avoided exposure to roaming bands of murderers and thieves where their very lives were at risk and, unbeknown to them, Rastus had a significant investment in their lives in mind as he kept them safe at the top of the hill because Rastus contained within the depth of his being a secret power with which only those of royal blood *may* be endowed, yet how it shows up is when he is in need of protecting others, because deep down Rastus is exactly like his name, *bristly, prickly*, and *pugnacious*, making his kindness and brave-heartedness harder to emerge, and the real proof of his royal blood shows as he is protecting the weak and vulnerable, so… *well…* who would think a dachshund and rat terrier, the very Jack and Jill, could or would be vulnerable except that the truth is they really are since, you see, the dachshund called Jill (*Glimpses* is her nickname) has only three legs because of something that happened from a horrible encounter with a badger during a hunt, although never did anyone think a badger could hang onto a leg the way it did when she turned to fight back as it sank its razor sharp teeth into that front leg literally shearing it off at the first shoulder joint, and it was then that Rastus found Glimpses and dragged her back to the castle from the meadow where Jack watched through tear-filled eyes and Rastus sensed there was more here than just to separate two dogs who hunt or play, for these dogs were part of a union known to others as the "Rat Pack", and Rastus could tell he needed to save them from destruction, so he threw Glimpses onto his back and gave a bark of direction for Jack to follow their lengthy trek up the mountain to the castle where, unbeknown to all, Rastus' secret power was to be revealed as he magically shed his fur coat to reveal *hands*, not just any hands, but hands that seemed to grow out from his stomach, embedded with the tools and medicines he needed to repair the damage from the badger, and although Rastus was able to morph into this creature of great ability, he was not able to guarantee the wellness of the creature for whom he worked or toiled to the end of his extraordinary powers, and it did not seem to matter in the beginning, because it was only later that it became clear there simply was not enough energy to give the dog a healing, but that Glimpses needed a life of milk and honey, and the only way for that to happen was for them to leave on the pickup truck and travel into the unknown, along with Rastus who realized he had done all there was to do to help them, and it was time for them to learn that they have the strength within themselves to make their way to their future and find others with whom they could share the gift of safety and protection that they had gained from Rastus, the Royal Shih tzu. (689)

# Maddie and Tilly
## by Tronny Woodburn

I MET MADDIE AND TILLY AT THEIR BIRTHDAY CELEBRATION at the Rosy River Nursing Home a few years ago when they were both 85, lifetime friends, born just a few days apart, but as Maddie loved to tell everyone, "I'm the older one and Tilly's the baby sister I never had," and it was the day I learned their secret, five years later, after the party celebrating their 90th birthdays — oh, that was a bash, I tell you — when even though Maddie was confined to bed, she didn't miss out because Tilly insisted they wheel her downstairs for cake and ice cream that she enjoyed with great smiles, and after Tillie returned Maddie to their room, she joined me outside where we swung slowly back and forth on the porch swing for quite awhile, turning Tilly very quiet, as if her mind was somewhere else, until at length she began in a soft voice to tell me about a day she and Maddie were taking their walk in the park near where they lived and they stopped to rest on one of the benches, taking with them water bottles they had bought, when Maddie set hers down, and it fell over and rolled under the bench, and that's where they found what Tilly called "It" (yes, with a capital I), and paused for effect until I asked what they had found, and she responded that they weren't sure at first because they had only heard about such things, but they soon figured out they had found somebody's marijuana stash, "you know, pot... weed," she said and stopped to wait for my reaction which she got in short order when I asked what on earth It did, who did It belong to, and did someone come back for It, until Tilly chuckled a bit as she remembered, then told me very casually that they smoked It, again watching my reaction as I asked if they lit up right then and there and she said, no they went back home, to Maddie's house where they were living in those days, and she casually told me how they found the papers that her

late husband had used to roll cigarettes and they poured the pot
onto the papers and rolled themselves a couple of cigarettes,
which she remembered calling *reefers* or *joints*, and I
mentioned how they don't call them that anymore and asked
when this happened, and Tilly thought a moment before she
told me it was ten, maybe twelve years earlier, before they
moved into Rosy River, and then she pushed the swing with her
foot and we both fell into deep thoughts with her memories
and my surprise until I asked how It felt, and she perked up as
she related that she felt as if she were flying without a care in
the world and that all her aches and pains of growing old
disappeared and she called her "trip" amazing, rather *mind-
boggling*, and dear Tilly sat back and laughed at her pun, which
I didn't get at first, but I had to ask if they ever did It again and
she explained how they tried, even though It bothered their
lungs because Maddie had been a smoker when they were
young and while Tilly had not, It still bothered her breathing,
although they did try once or twice more, and when I asked
about the rest of the stash, because it sounded as if there was a
lot of the stuff, she calmly said they baked some of It into
brownies, which they had heard about, but they *tasted funny*,
and Tilly added another pun, telling me they *felt funny*, and she
laughed again, gradually lowering her voice to a quiet hum as
we rocked back and forth on the porch swing until I asked
again about the rest of the stash... but at that moment we were
interrupted by a nurse who came out onto the porch and sat
down in a nearby chair, reached over and solemnly took Tilly's
hand as she intoned, "it's over", meaning that Maddie seemed
to have succumbed, probably an hour or so earlier after we
came down to the porch, but the nurse didn't think she
suffered, and Tilly, looking sad, her eyes glossy with tears, but
with a half-smile on her lips, leaned over and whispered to me,
"She didn't." (730)

# Dear Mr. Luccarelli
## by Sara Jacobelli

DEAR MR. LUCCARELLI,
  You might wonder why I'm writing you this letter, but the truth is I write you a letter every day… no it's not a love note or a crush note or anything like that… but I really do like you a lot, maybe more than I should since you're my English teacher and I'm only twelve (almost thirteen) but anyhow, I have a lot to tell you, and I just want you to know that I sometimes ride my bike by your house and I see you sitting up late by yourself so I wondered where's your wife and then my mom said she heard a rumor that you and Mrs. Luccarelli were Getting Divorced, but my mom drinks a lot and she says a lot of mean crap when she's drunk, so I don't know if that's true or not, but I just want you to know that I think you're a really good dad and I remember when you told us you ordered a pizza every Friday night and your family played games and ate pizza and you called it Family Game Night and I said, "Oh yeah we do that at my house too," but… well I was lying because we never did that Not Once and I remember you said that you always did stuff with your little boy's Cub Scout troop and you went to all your little girl's soccer games and I just think you are the Best Father and the Best Husband ever ever ever and your wife is Horrible if she doesn't love you anymore, which brings me to my idea, which is what I was thinking, you know, that my mom was only sixteen when she married my pop and he was a million years older than her, and since you're thirty-three and pretty soon I'm going to be thirteen, so if you're interested, maybe when I'm sixteen and you're thirty-six we could get Married and I just can't wait to move out and get away from my mom and my brothers fighting all the time and I think your kids are so cute and we could have more kids too, and in the meantime maybe I could babysit for you if your wife

moves out, and I could even move in and be the nanny like they have nannies on TV and in the movies, like I could just live there and stuff, but anyhow, it's just an idea and don't worry about my father shooting you if you marry me since my father is going back to prison soon anyway so he won't bother you because he got busted for selling drugs again and he was on probation so now he's back in jail waiting to be sent "up the river" my mom said... oh, and if you want to know, I have two questions, which are a) am I in love with you and b) why did I fall in love with you, and that's easy because the answer to question a) is yes yes yes, and as for question b) when you came to see me at the hospital after I got hit by a car, I just couldn't believe that a teacher could care that much, and there you were, Italian just like me but with black hair and blue eyes instead of brown hair and brown eyes, and I looked at those blue eyes and your crooked smile and your suit was kinda wrinkled and there you were visiting me and you brought me books and you said I was so smart and I was the best writer and speller in your class, even though you said I'm not that good at Punctuation, but you Winked when you said it, and my own father didn't even bother to come visit me, but you did, so if your wife doesn't appreciate you, you can just tell her Goodbye and you and me can raise those cute kids together and I can dress them in cute little outfits and people might not understand but maybe I can become a teacher too just like you and we can move away from here, and I hope you like cats because I want to bring my cats, Bonnie and Clyde, with me, but we can talk about that later, and I hope your Heart isn't broken about Getting a Divorce but my mom says there's worse things than Divorce, love, love love, Maria "Marty" Riccio,
XOXOXO.
(751)

# Nigel's Gift
## by Judy Ashley

*E*IGHT-YEAR-OLD NIGEL LEFT EARLY FOR SCHOOL because he always seemed to get sidetracked along the way, and today was no different as he sauntered down the sidewalk swishing his long stick and kicking rocks, cans, or anything else lying in his path while mumbling to himself *I know Dad likes Colin better than me cuz Colin's got lots of trophies cuz he's really good in sports and Dad's always saying, "you are destined for the major leagues, Colin", like all he cares about is sports and trophies and stuff like that*, but Nigel didn't share his brother's athletic ability nor did he have his sister Shelby's musical talent — she could bring listeners to tears or rowdy excitement when her long fingers magically glided over the piano keys — but *what can I do to make Dad proud of me*, he thought when Mrs. Brown called out to him as he came upon her house, "Good Morning Nigel," to which he replied, "Good Morning, Mrs. Brown, that's a real pretty dress you're wearing today," as he gave her his great big signature smile not knowing that she came outside every day at this time just so she could see Nigel's smile and hear his greeting, which always warmed her heart and made it a little easier for her to get through her day, which was difficult since her husband of forty-five years had recently passed away and, as Nigel continued on his way, he came upon old Mr. Tom trying to hook the garden hose up to the faucet with his old creaky, shaky hands, and the boy asked, "Need some help, Mr. Tom?" as he walked through the gate and headed toward Mr. Tom and gently took hold of the hose and screwed it onto the faucet just like his dad had taught him, and said, "There you go, Mr. Tom, see you later," and he continued on his way as Mr. Tom called after him, "You're a good boy Nigel, and thanks for the help," smiling back at Nigel who was wearing that big warm smile of his that ran from ear to ear while he thought to himself how much he looked forward to Nigel's daily momentary visits, and as Nigel continued walking toward school he saw his classmate, Eloise, sitting on the curb crying and naturally, Nigel asked her what was wrong and she sobbed that she'd dropped her homework into the grate where it got caught in the bars and now she was going to be in so much trouble, but Nigel immediately told her it was no problem while he used his stick to dislodge her papers from the grate and handed them to her saying, "They're a little dirty but you can brush them off and then you won't be in trouble with Teacher," for which Eloise thanked Nigel with, "You saved my life," to which Nigel replied, "Ah, it was nothing, see ya around," while he continued on his way thinking about how he wished he could be really smart like his other sister, Lizabeth, who knew everything and who was getting a big scholarship for college because she was so smart and then Dad would be really proud of him, and as Nigel turned the corner, he heard Mrs. Oliver's little dog whimpering and saw that the dog had gotten itself all tangled up in the rope again, so Nigel climbed over the short fence and when he got Mrs. Oliver's dog all straightened out, it promptly jumped up excitedly with its tail wagging as if turbo charged, gratefully licking Nigel's face, to which the boy answered, "I better go tell Mrs. Oliver she forgot to bring you in the house with her," after which Nigel continued on his way to school trying to think about ways he could make his dad proud of him, but he just didn't know how because he wasn't like his brother and sisters — he was different — *but I'll just keep thinking on it* he said to himself, *there must be something I'm good at,* and Nigel kept on thinking about ways he could make his dad proud while he continued to help those in distress and continued to bring a little joy into the lives of those whom he met along his way, not realizing how very proud his dad already was of the little boy with the million dollar smile that could melt a glacier and who, with his selfless spirit, spread so much kindness every day in many small, ordinary ways to so many different people, never knowing how many lives he touched nor how many people had warmly etched his memory forever into their hearts as Nigel continued to meander on his way through life. (793)

# Need Help? Just Ask
## by Jennifer Schneider

*A*S I SAT DOWN AND WOKE MY SLEEPY BUT LOYAL even if overworked computer, a new email alert chirped with its usually crisp, high-pitched tone that often disguised, or at least distorted, the nature of the underlying communication which reads: "Dear Instructor: I realize, regrettably and with much dismay and embarrassment that this might seem to you to be somewhat of a predictable correspondence, but I assure you that I am writing with my deepest regrets and my, once again, true and sincere surprise, to let you know that my assignment will be late for a variety of unfortunate circumstances, each of which I assure you is utterly and entirely unavoidable, out of my control, and without any possible means of prevention and, for your benefit and review, clearly delineated and explained down to the finest of detail, and that is because I was initially delayed due to a ferocious and fierce headache that emerged in remarkably splendid force after I attended my fourth youngest sibling's introductory band concert where the students were enthusiastic beginners who failed to understand the honestly quite remarkable power of their own windpipes, especially when compared with the relative size of their bodies and the room in which they performed, and then next, my cat fell asleep on my laptop and accidentally deleted all of the text in my fifth and almost final version of my draft for our course project, and third, my adorably precocious but a bit too curious pet gerbil (at a mere six weeks of age) discovered the power of his paw and enjoyed some rigorous exercise that sadly resulted in a most unfortunate need to reboot my computer only to discover my draft had not been satisfactorily saved, and fourth, my older sister (I am one of eight children — yes, eight! — and we all use the same computer) who for the most part is not all that bad and actually quite endearing, suddenly remembered that she too had an important assignment that required use of our family's sole laptop for the period of time that most unfortunately fell at precisely the same (already delayed three times) block of time I had dedicated for my own school work, and fifth, my youngest brother unexpectedly needed help tying his shoes and somehow made a game of repeatedly untying what I had just tied, which brings me to sixth, which involves my youngest sister, who had a tooth that had wiggled for so long that it finally fell out and dropped, most unfortunately, into my dog's water bowl and I had to rush to save the tooth (and my dog's digestive system), then seventh, and most upsetting of all, despite all of these challenges, I was amazingly about to submit my work with time to spare and then, for no apparent reason, my poodle barked (I'd insist he *howled* if I hadn't already disclosed that he was a poodle) louder than ever before, maybe because he was mad that I rescued the tooth, which startled my baby brother who screamed in alarm, and the piercing sound of his wail made my third oldest sibling turn too quickly and as a result she tripped and accidentally pulled and tore the electrical cord which was powering our Internet and that's when I asked my second oldest sibling to rush me to the library so that I could use their Wifi, and we drove as quickly as legally permitted but had to pull over to let a circus pass (who knew these were still a thing), and by the time we finally reached the library the clock had just struck eleven o'clock and the doors were automatically locked, which make this a regretful explanatory correspondence and my official notice of a late submission that, most remarkably given the circumstances and my relentless string of bad luck, I have managed to submit a mere two seconds before the clock has struck our midnight deadline according to the fine print, which, I might add, is so fine that I might have easily missed it if not for the luck of having my twin sister unexpectedly discover this important detail when she was searching for her own homework in my stack of papers and, as you know, makes the formal deadline for alerting you of an exigent circumstance

in my hometown, miles away from yours but close in my heart,
Fondly, Your ever-grateful, always well-intentioned and
eternally late Student" and when I had read it, I replied once
more, and as I always do, "Please, just ask when you need some
more time, because after all the unpredictability of our lives,
time will always be one of the most challenging and also the
most rewarding parts of achieving your educational goals, so
please — just ask,
Your Very Patient Instructor."
(803)

# Pooped
## by Terry Sager

*I*T WAS A CRAZY MORNING, AND I'M POOPED — but now the foster kittens are sleeping and they've been fed, their litter boxes cleaned, their water dish filled, and we played kitten games until finally, one by one they gave into sleep and became a pile of fluff, ears, and whiskers, blending together, creating a living, breathing fur blanket, and although I doubt much could wake them right now, I tip-toe out of the room, because although it's the most amazing feeling to walk into a room and be charged by five little fluffy beasts who must think I'm their mom because they were just tiny when they lost their real mom, I need to get away for a while, yes, I decide, I will go to the mall, and although it's not my usual form of escape, I actually do need another pair of jeans (of course you do), and a dose of commercialism, a short escape into the "real" world for a while, and as just one last thing to do before I escape, I go outside to call in the dogs, taking a minute to walk on the newly formed blanket of fallen leaves of orange, yellow, and red, that have formed their own special blanket in my yard, and as I let the dogs in, they run past me to their dishes to their breakfast, and as much as I love all the creatures in my care, I really am in total need of a break, to get the heck out of the house and do something totally selfish, like shopping, and since the holiday crowds are weeks away, and the mall parking lot is mostly empty, and I really *do* need a new pair of jeans, and maybe some other stuff, and there are all kinds of sales, so this is going to be fun, and I actually find what I'm looking for, in my size (I think), but since I am not a big fan of shopping, and even a lesser fan of returns, I make myself go to the dressing room and kick off my waterproof slip-on shoes, which I wear a lot in the rainy season, try on the jeans which are a size smaller than I usually wear, which I know has to be a retail trick because I know I have not lost a pound lately, but they fit and I feel a bit of elation — this is going to be a cool shopping trip — but nearly as soon as that little bit of optimism strikes, I put my old jeans back on and as I start to slip on my super-sexy rubber shoes, I see the edges of colorful fall leaves sticking out from the side of the right one, and I wonder how that could be since the parking lot was totally clear of any kind of foliage, and as I continue to wonder how those leaves could possibly be affixed to the bottom of my shoe, the proverbial light comes on, and I look and see, yes, the glue is dog poop, and yet, I cannot smell anything rotten, and ask myself how could I have been in the closed space of my car and not smell that familiar smell, and then shop for another twenty minutes and *then*, in the confines of the dressing room, still with no odor, and my first thought is that I must get out of there and get this cleaned off my shoes, and then my brain, says, no, if you can't smell it, no one else can, or maybe they can, but I really don't care, and I really am finished shopping, and I am ready to go home and so I go to the check-out and hope for a really fast transaction, but of course, no, that isn't going to happen, because although there is only one person in front of me, she is returning seven items and buying three, and the clerk is obviously new, but at least I am still not smelling anything and they don't seem to either, and I wonder if something is wrong with me that, rather than ask the salesperson to hold my soon-to-be-purchases and go out into the parking lot and take care of the problem, I decide to stay in line, not really even having the energy to explain the situation, because what if the person I hand them to goes on break or something, and then the other one puts them back or something, so there I am, waiting to pay for my finds, with poop on my shoe, now feeling like my little shopping trip has not really gotten me away from the nitty-gritty of caring for animals, because I brought the nitty-gritty with me, on my shoe, and I have to admit, with a smile, yes, and perhaps just a tad touched in the head, yes, I am indeed, pooped... (824)

# Spider
## by Debbie Davidson

*I*T WAS ONE OF THOSE DAYS SINCE HIS BIRTH that the tiny brown spider dared to venture away from his mother and siblings, but for curiosity's sake and for the dream he had, he couldn't help himself from wanting to leave the comfort of his family, and besides he liked exploring and especially the enormous barn he had been born in and practically raised all of the 150 or so days he had been alive and feeling like he wanted to just get away from all those other brown spiders who looked just like him, and sometimes he couldn't tell himself apart from the others and that was not acceptable in his world or mind because his aim in life was not just to be a disgusting spider, it was to be a spider who was cherished for his good looks — and those he had — and he was determined to show the world that although he was a spider, a brown recluse spider, nonetheless he was good-looking and would never harm anybody, besides he despised that most people didn't like his species since spiders had more reasons to not like people, after all, for people were a heck of a lot bigger and some a lot uglier than spiders, but he wasn't sure people, especially women, would see his beauty the way he did, and that bothered him, which is why he set out to leave the safety of his mom, brothers, and sisters to meet the little girl his mother had told them about who lives in the house across from the barn, so he decided he would do the unthinkable, he would talk to her, yes, talk, a talking brown recluse spider, talking and making sense to people — now that would make the headlines if he could pull this off — and he hoped he could talk to her about his idea without frightening her because fear could cause his whole plan to fail and possibly end his life on this earth, but he couldn't worry about that right now because he had to first find his way safely out of the barn, then into the house where the little girl's family lived (Andy the father, Linda the mother, Miles the only boy and oldest child, Eloise the girl he wanted to talk to, and Brea the cry baby), almost 200 yards from the barn, but unfortunately, there were lots of obstacles along the path to her house, although his destiny urged him on since his earth-shattering revelation could alter the way people and spiders interact, and that thought both excited and encouraged him to take the first step, and although he knew he had to be careful ensuring he arrived unharmed at his history-making destination which wasn't really that far away from where he was now, but only outside the barn door, and, boy, did that fresh air feel good to the fine hair on his legs and across his face as he stealthily raced through the tall grass feeling exhilarated because he sensed the girl would love him when she saw him up close and he couldn't wait to watch her face when he started talking to explain his history-making idea, which he felt confident would entice her to help him because Eloise needed something to boost her self-confidence since Brea had long ago figured out how to keep her parent's attention by crying loudly and often, which didn't work for Eloise, so she needed his brilliant idea, and if she could be enticed to see him the way he saw himself, perhaps girls and women all over the world would cease to be afraid of spiders and they could cohabit without fear and, yes, as the smaller of the two, spiders run from people because they don't want to get crushed or sprayed with Raid, and every spider knows instinctively they are perceived as a threat because most people think they are ugly and this spider is taking people on, and they will see his beauty and listen to his appeal to treat spiders with dignity because spiders need love too, so he continued toward the house dodging two chained-up barking dogs, the curious cat Mandy who was playing with a dead bird, Andy as he backed his car out of the driveway, and a host of other life-threatening obstacles as the little spider raced toward the house, and when he reached it, the tiny spider rapidly spun his web to climb along the side of the house to avoid detection, and when he spotted Eloise inside her room, he excitedly cruised down through a small hole in the wall and spun his web in front of her as close as he could get without notice, admiringly plotting his introduction, when Eloise unexpectedly screamed, "SPIDER," causing him to run as fast as he could down his web and hide under her bed still hearing her screaming, and encouraged to do what he planned from the moment he stepped outside the barn, he spoke, and he realized speaking totally frightened her to the point she used super-human strength to throw off the top mattress, then the box spring from her bed, and spotting him, she grabbed her size six-and-a-half-inch shoe and whacked him several times in succession before he lay, splattered, unrecognizable as a spider, then she picked up his pieces with a tissue and flushed them down the toilet... (912)

# Dotty's Boys
## by Ruth Anderson

*Bachelor Officers' Quarters (BOQ) 203*
*Grayson Air Force Base, August 4, 1968*

D OTTY COLES, HEAD HOUSEKEEPER, ARMS FULL of dirty sheets, pushed open the swinging doors leading to the basement laundry room, gasped, dropped the sheets, and cautiously approached the sprawled figure of Major Giles Jackson, whose head was oddly twisted against the base of the concrete washtub, and she knew he was dead before she gently pushed at him with her shoe before backing into a basket of laundry that she recognized belonged to Captain Matt Gibbons, and she knew instantly what had happened, but she would never reveal the likely avenger because Major Jackson had been the rudest, crudest man she'd ever met, sneaking up on people to scare them, finding fault, leaving explicit pornography where he knew she'd see it, and otherwise ignoring her except for the monthly check he was obliged to leave in his room with never one penny more than was owed, unlike Gibbons and all the others who often gave her tips or boxes of candy and the like, no, not Jackson who was a creep who preyed on young officers, and she reasoned that Gibbons had come down with his laundry and Jackson had pounced on him, and Gibbons fought back, so that when Jackson fell, his head hit the concrete and that was that, and good riddance, though one shouldn't speak ill of the dead, for now instead she had to think how to protect Gibbons before she called the base security police, for Gibbons, who had finished his flight training, was due to fly to Vietnam in about a month, and she knew how ready he was to go and do his duty as a fighter pilot, though she would gladly have kept him here as she would all of "her boys" excluding Jackson, who somehow had kept himself from going off to war, and so she first scoured the washtub inside and out and both sides of the swinging door, and then she picked up the laundry basket and took it up to Gibbon's room and placed it on his bed, so that he would know that she was protecting him, and then she returned downstairs and called the security police, who came quickly, verified the death, and proceeded to launch an investigation that eventually led to Dotty's interrogation by a legal officer named Lieutenant Colonel Denforth, a kind, but probing officer, who sought her opinion on what she had found and asked why they found no fingerprints on the door or the washtub, and had to accept her explanation of having scoured them the day before, although she suspected it was obvious the door was still damp but without fingerprints, and when all occupants denied any knowledge, the case went cold, and then just before he shipped out, Gibbons asked her to come to his room where he gave her a sizeable tip and a sealed envelope that he said she was to give to the legal office if he were killed in the war, and she knew she had been right, and she put the letter in her safe deposit box at the bank and got on with her life, made more pleasant by the absence of Major Jackson, until she received the devastating word from Denforth in February that Gibbons' plane had gone down, and it was certain that he did not survive, and was there anything she wanted to tell the legal team now that Gibbons was very likely dead, so after two sleepless nights, she retrieved the sealed letter and reluctantly took it to Denforth who opened and read it, asked if she knew what it contained, which she honestly did not, then told her she was close to being an accessory to murder and had best not mention the letter ever to anyone, which she had no intention of doing, and she withdrew to mourn the loss of the captain, grateful for Denforth's compassion, until he came looking for her at the BOQ to report that Gibbons had not died, but was in fact a prisoner of war, whereupon Dotty's hands flew to her face in pleasure at the news, until her second thought was about what would happen next to both Gibbons and to her, which question she might have verbalized but didn't, because the next minute, Denforth was gently pressing Gibbons' resealed envelope into her hand, noting with solemnity that Gibbons was paying his dues and nothing further need be said, which was the case until it came to be that the prisoners were released in 1973, and in April, Dotty heard her name being called in the upstairs hallway, and when she stepped out of the room she was tending, there stood a much older Captain Gibbons, arms held wide, and she flew into them, patting him and blessing him as she had every evening in her prayers, and he was giving her another envelope and thanking her for saving his life, and she pulled him into the room and told him what had happened, and they both cried a little, and then he was off to his new assignment in Europe, and she looked inside the new envelope to find a very substantial check, whereupon she sat down in the middle of the bed, tears running down her cheeks, because two days earlier she had learned that her daughter who lived with her Air Force husband in Japan was pregnant with Dotty's first grandchild, and now she could afford to fly there when the baby came, and oh God was good, and finally she could whisper "rest in peace, Major Jackson, rest in peace." (946)

# The Oak
## by Jude Roy

*T*HE OAK STOOD OVER TWO HUNDRED YEARS OLD, a sapling when Native Americans brushed up against it stalking the wild bison that roamed the southern prairies, a young tree when the first Cajuns arrived pushing back the red man, a survivor of the ax while its brothers and sisters were felled and used to build houses, barns, wagons, tools and make way for the farms they would build, standing tall when Denis Boudreaux built the first public building, a combination jail and meeting house, a shack made from rough-hewn cypress boards from trees harvested in the Bayou des Sauvages Swamp just north of the swelling community, stood there when Denis and his son Jean tacked up the sign over the door, BOUDREAUXVILLE, stood there as a small group gathered for the event, set up tables under the shade of the oak and celebrated with alcohol, food, and music, stood there when a young man in a frock coat, the first Ellison — Daniel Demetrius Ellison — rode into town on a shiny black mare, stood there when Mr. Ellison introduced the cotton gin to the town, stood there to watch the town swell to three hundred residents, erect two taverns, two grocery stores, and several other retail businesses, stood there when Demetrius added a cotton press and a warehouse on the banks of Bayou des Sauvages, stood there to witness every man, woman, and child pitch in to till the prairie land and plant cotton to take to Mr. Ellison's gin, stood there to watch as the government came in and dredged Bayou des Sauvages to accommodate the barges loaded down with cotton bales that eventually made their way to New Orleans and then on to the Carolinas and the great textile mills in the east, stood there when young boys stripped naked and swam the muddy waters of Bayou des Sauvages, stood there as old men sat on overturned buckets, fishing the bayou for catfish, *sac au lait,* and gar, stood there when the rains came and the bayou flooded her banks, depositing mineral-rich silt which the townspeople and the farmers saw as a necessary inconvenience, stood there as the farmers relied more and more on commercial fertilizers and viewed the flooding as something that needed correcting, stood there when the Army Corps of Engineers came in and built a levee along the bayou to stop the flooding, stood there when the townspeople, in appreciation for all Daniel Ellison had done for the town, renamed it Ellisonville, painted the cypress meetinghouse white, and hung up another sign over its door, which read, ELLISONVILLE, stood there three years later when the meetinghouse burned down, stood there to hear the frantic cries of the three prisoners inside and saw their charred remains carried out and buried in the cemetery on the hill in unmarked graves, stood there when the town rebuilt the meetinghouse, called it a *courthouse* then, bigger this time, painted it white, and added a column or two to differentiate it from the other buildings in the town, stood there when the tornado of 1907 left only the columns standing, stood there when Mr. Ellison's son, David Demitrius, contacted an architect from New England to design a new building that would dwarf in size and appearance anything in that area, stood there when the Cajun contractor tried to follow the Greek revival blueprint, stood there to watch the building turn into a combination of Greek revival and Cajun practical, one building with four shotgun-styled sections, the only thing the local carpenters had experience building, stood there when the town grew to a thousand residents, then two thousand, then ten thousand and became the parish seat, stood there to grow older, its branches thick and moss-covered, stood there as the townspeople set up tables and blankets under its protective branches and danced, drank, ate, and in their soft nasal French talked about love, politics, and cotton, stood there as the town grew even larger, the crowds bigger, the music louder, the language less French and more English, stood there when the American teachers came in and punished the little Cajun children for speaking French in the classrooms and on the school grounds, whittling away at the language until it all but disappeared and the Cajuns were no more unique than the Americans to the north of them, stood there when electricity lit up the dark skies, when tar and then pavement covered the streets as horses were replaced by cars, stood there when the trains rumbled across the town, the tracks leading straight to the cotton gin, eliminating the need for the warehouse on the bayou and the barges, stood there when Daniel Ellison's great-great-grandson, Peter D. Ellison, turned the warehouse into a successful restaurant, stood there to see the train tracks provide a natural boundary between the town's rich and poor, black and white, stood there when the grocery stores turned into supermarkets, *fais do dos* were no longer good enough for people, and they turned to dance halls, and when used car lots took up whole blocks and doctors became politicians, who with one hand helped the people and with the other robbed them, stood there when six hooded men hung the young black musician for being nice to a white girl, stood there when the lumber companies ravaged Bayou des Sauvages Swamp of all the old-growth cypress, watched them drain the swamp and turn it into cotton fields, rice fields, and later, soybean fields, stood there when the farmers started using poisons to rid their crops of the boll weevils and other insects, stood there to watch the poisons make their way into Bayou des Sauvages, to watch the dead fish float in long slow-moving lines during poison season, to watch the cancer rate rise, to watch parents prevent their children from swimming in the bayou, to watch townspeople refuse to eat fish caught in the bayou, to watch the deadly muddy water move slowly past the town like the passing of life, stood there for all this, and from its vantage point become the history of Ellisonville, there to mark time with every scar on its woody exterior, every initial carved in its tough hide, and every ring running through its living core, and still it stands... (1052)

# Taxi Dancers
## by Val Dumond

T HE GIRLS WERE NEVER SURE WHERE THE LIMO CAME FROM, but they were soon to remember all they learned the day they first heard the song called "Taxi Dancers", a ditty recalling sounds of Abba but obviously meant for them, the five who were picked up that day shortly after they were graduated from high school, beginning with Scamp, a mischievous young lady who hung out near the taxi stands at the bus station where she was looking for someone fun to entertain her for the day, and continuing as the limo found Ginger Peachy, the gorgeous ingénue, haunting the theaters early looking for a role in the next musical, proceeding to Rosy Freckles, the exact opposite of beauty but owning the kind of fascination where you don't know what she'll do next, and moving on to find Flossie, a rather properly staid young woman who lived in a rather properly staid brownstone flat and was properly waiting as the limo pulled up, climbed inside, and waved for the driver to continue to pick up the last of them, Jo who was sitting outside a Wall Street skyscraper waiting for the offices to open and who eagerly asked the driver if breakfast was in the offing, which it was, responded the driver as they pulled into line at a pickup station to load a variety breakfast into the limo, which then pulled away as the girls dug into the food as the limo radio continued to play that song, "Taxi Dancers", over and over until the girls began to hum along, with Rose, the first to memorize all the lyrics and coach the others as they quickly grasped onto the catchy words, something about a taxi dancer, which the girls didn't understand since they didn't know what a taxi dancer was, but they were soon to find out, as the limousine drove slowly through Central Park, allowing the girls to enjoy the quiet of nature as they munched on cinnamon rolls and sipped their coffee, before noticing that the limo had sped up a bit and was leaving the park, heading for… they didn't know, although each of them had lived all their lives in Manhattan, the center of their world which had taken a turn toward excitement for them as they wondered, some asking aloud, "Where are we going now?" without an answer from the driver, only a kind of nod that said "everything will be made clear", and the girls whispered to each other their thoughts as to why they had been chosen for whatever adventure this was, why that song was being played over and over, until someone, probably Flossie, suggested it was a promotional scheme to announce a new song, something a few production companies often used to introduce a new album or a musician of some kind, a singer, a band, or instrumentalist, but she wasn't sure, to which Scamp suggested they were being kidnapped for ransom, which made everyone laugh because none of them came from rich families, although Jo knew a lot about finances and probably would be rich one day, but that was speculation, much like the group's speculation about the limo, the song, and each other, which prompted them to share more of their personal information among themselves, everything from telling of their particular interests and why they chose them to sharing family connections (for those who had families to share), and, in short, spending the afternoon in pleasant conversation until the limo made another stop, this one not for a traffic light but for a parking spot in front of a… "it's a ballroom!" shouted Ginger Peachy as she recognized the dance hall where auditions often were held and where she now watched the limo driver shut off the engine, get out of the vehicle, and come around to open the door for them, indicating this was their destination, and waving them inside, where they looked around the dimly lit hall and… yes, it was definitely the same music they heard then, the tune they had been listening to all day, and they broke into song, performing the words perfectly and garnering the attention of passers-by, most of them gentlemen awaiting a dancing partner, and there they were, five talented, vivacious girls who looked ready to dance, and dance they did, Scamp finding ways to show her partner how to double-step and spin to the music, and Ginger Peachy choosing to glide waltz-like with her partner, and Rosy Freckles who did a kind of jitterbug step and followed her partner's clues to add some gymnastics as well, as Flossie who watched them enviously wishing she could add more to her dancing than just... dancing, but it was Jo who intrigued her as she tried to take the lead away from her gentleman partner, unsuccessful for the first few tries, then actually leading him to the style she wanted to dance, much like her cohorts, all dancing their own styles their own ways and having a heck of a lot of fun at the same time, all the while humming and sometimes singing aloud the lyrics to this tune, as the crowd watched for a time before joining in with them, all of which lasted a couple of fun hours before the limousine driver reappeared and signaled to the riders that it was time to go, mentioning that dinner was about to be served at a very high-end restaurant, upon which announcement the girls objected furiously and demanded something more mundane, hamburgers maybe, or Chinese takeout, or even... and that's what they all agreed upon... pizza, real New York pizza, which is exactly what they enjoyed to cap off their evening before they piled back into the limo, took up singing their song again, and headed back to where they came from, beginning with Scamp, who was let off at the bus station, Ginger Peachy at her walk-up flat she shared in the theater district, Rosy Freckles who lived with her grandmother in one of those buildings they used to call "tenements", Flossy at her brownstone, and Jo at a rather showy posh-looking apartment building, which she hurriedly explained by telling the driver she didn't rent an apartment, but only worked there in the maintenance department, which would have surprised the others if they had been there, but Jo was the last to be dropped off before the limo pulled away, disappearing back into the New York evening traffic and oblivion, but remaining in the memory of the five girls who had been picked up that morning, wondering where the limo came from and why it played only one song — "Taxi Dancers" — but then, what better way was there to announce a brand new song than to promote it with a jazzy bunch of girls who would make it popular throughout New York, and believe me, that is exactly what happened. (1151)

# Please, Just Listen
## by Jennifer Schneider

A S AN AGING AND OFTEN STUBBORNLY PROUD (or *proudly stubborn*, depending on who is doing the talking) Clyde Bernard, after composing himself and collecting his sometimes scattered thoughts, sat at his battered, very well-worn, memory-laden kitchen table in a dimly lit room on the 54th floor of a 100-year-old apartment building on the Upper West Side (you'd never guess the luck Clyde struck when he found the apartment nestled on a street an almost equidistant stone's throw from Zabar's and Barney Greengrass where a warm welcome — and a wait — is a given) of New York City and typed his original response, neither restricted by character limits nor motivated by the possibility of re-tweets (despite the inexplicably fleeting joy they often yielded), likes, or up-posts, to the unexpectedly provocative and somehow refreshing (even in these days, soon to be years, more typically characterized and dominated by exhaustion and weariness provoked and sustained by 24-hour news, incessant tweets, and relentless tragedy) classroom prompts that inquire and truly seek students' honest views, personal experiences, and reflections (they really want to know? thought Clyde) about the interactions between and intersections of social justice, social media, and social relations and relationships more generally... and as a normally shy and hesitant Suzanna Williams was devouring a self-indulging (and surprisingly delicious) meal of aged cheese, spicy cheddar and fire-roasted veggie multi-grain crackers and overly-ripe (her absolute favorite) bananas as she edited and revised (for no less than eight times in a span of time that consumed no less than 80 minutes) her initial (if not at first impulsive) highly emotional, highly engaged (if not highly enraged) thoughts and reactions to the same prompt, to produce a carefully revised, edited, and ultimately, much to

Suzanna's delight, well-articulated and strongly-supported final piece of writing before submitting to the virtual forums via a keyboard perched on a linoleum counter at a 24-hour diner (you know the kind, where the coffee is always brewing but never quite hot and the conversation never stops) in the middle of a Luxembourg neighborhood situated somehow at an almost equidistant location, when travel time is calculated by car, to any of Germany, Belgium, or France... and as Stella Schmitz, a (usually) perky and eager want-to-be world traveler with a fondness for black and white movies, romance novels, and Hollywood Boulevard, but seemingly forever destined to be an on-call waitress (nothing wrong with that, Stella constantly tells herself) and struggling actor (forever the bridesmaid, never the bride, and always available for a call-back, but rarely the recipient of a gig) who secretly lives paycheck-to-paycheck on a good week, but never stops smiling with her bright red-painted lips, was on break in a similar 24-hour diner (with much stronger coffee and a deep-dish pecan pie that should have put the best U.S. Southern diners and New York City delis on alert for a leaked recipe) as she regrouped, edited, vigorously revised, and eloquently composed her own thoughts and written response because she suddenly found her often-unexplainable ideas and quasi-political/personal opinions could, instead of the often counter-productive reactions of either indifference or anger, be used to support, strengthen, and develop a common if not united understanding... and while the usually reserved Cliff (a craftsman who spent years working the production lines for a Fortune 500 company while somehow managing to amass a hefty dose of skepticism and what turned out to be the polar opposite of a fortune) was simultaneously and quite surprisingly singing (to an upbeat tune and with an upbeat tone) along with his radio during his mid-afternoon break at the factory while avidly conducting online research (thanks to Wifi that usually worked) and carefully constructing his fifth — no make that his sixth — example (well matched to his six decades of lived experiences) to share as support for his well-articulated concerns to a classroom post shared moments earlier (albeit on the other side of the world) on the same topic by... Selamaa Halem, a vibrant and resilient young woman who, despite challenges no one should ever have to face or overcome, yearned for an education and possessed a determination to break all local barriers and expectations as she fought with all she knew for opportunities many of us have long taken for granted yet, somehow, too often find insufficient despite the comparable plethora of luxuriousness bestowed upon many others by these often-overlooked and underappreciated fortuitous gems of fortune, situated squarely across the globe and though multiple time zones away from the typing fingers of her classmates... including Xi Xou (a single dad stationed in Germany, determined to make a better life for his young daughter)... and Charmanee Jacobs (a single mom from Brazil determined to do the same for her two young sons)... and William Sternish (a respected Marine determined to obtain a degree to support his transition to civilian life), among a host of others, was making the most of a sleepless night with her oh-so-adorable but seemingly never tired and always hungry newborn by reading along with the stream of posts shared over the past 24 hours, the virtual classroom forum was alive and lit with respectfully thoughtful debate and discussion, the energy and passion almost tangible across the digital airwaves and throughout the far reaches of the globe that the course students call home, it almost seemed, if not only for a virtual moment that somehow sustained itself well beyond the more typical (or at least more common of recent days) flicker of hope that fades as quickly as a melting candle, that hope persists, that we can, we will, continue to fight for what we believe, and continue to debate honestly, respectfully, and passionately for our dreams, our beliefs, our values, and our aspirations, while at the same time truly listening to and respecting those same and often conflicting dreams, beliefs, values, and aspirations of others, so that it almost seems possible that those who have never met face to face, yet have come to know one another as thoughtful, caring, and inquisitive human beings with surprisingly similar challenges through educational interactions can, could, and would protect the hope that is our future, and that our future is the one we have long hoped for, as I choose to believe — like Clyde, Suzanna, Stella, Cliff, Selamaa, Xi, Charmanee and Will — that if a virtual classroom can unite and encourage reflection, respect, and even change among a patchwork of strong, dignified, and wildly-different individuals, generations, nationalities, genders, and races, then maybe… yes maybe… through sharing, reflecting, reflecting some more, listening, truly listening, clarifying, debating, sharing, and (most of all) listening to learn, understand, and appreciate, tomorrow not only can, but will indeed, be better than today… so that I too took a chance and voiced virtually and digitally, to my surprise and also my delight, my suddenly infinitely more optimistic perspective on our collective future and, before signing off for my night (but my classmates' day), I clicked Enter, promised to always listen (and not simply hear) and asked, if I could have but one wish, that everyone else do the same — listen, please, just listen. (1194)

# I Wish I'd Been Mrs. Noah Webster
## by Val Dumond

P ICTURE NOAH WEBSTER CRAWLING OUT OF BED, scratching himself, yawning and stretching, then stopping in mid-stretch as the thought hits him that with folks talking independence, the day people can decide what they *want* to read and write, and continuing with the idea that if this reading and writing thing catches on, folks will need a book to learn from, an American book, which he believes he could put together, maybe even use American words, such as *skunk* and *squash*, and he can collect all the words so's folks will be ready when the time comes, because he's fed up using British textbooks for his students like the one he wrote as (a spelling/pronunciation book when he was twenty-five and from which Ben Franklin's granddaughter learned to read), and the young man began to collect words the way Colonists spelled them, re-spelling many British words to reflect "the American way" (removing the "u" from the English *honour*, the "k" from words like *musick*, the "e" from *judgement*, and reversing the "re" in *centre*), planning to put them in the first American dictionary, and, oh yes, he took time out to marry Rebecca Greenleaf and start a family, but the forever scholar never forgot about his new dictionary, nor did his gracious wife, who — gee, I wish I had been there — because if I had been his wife, Rebecca Greenleaf Webster, I would have encouraged him to take a wider view of some words and a narrower view of others, asking him to make sure certain words maintained their original meaning, and I'd have asked him to call me by *my* name, not *his*, since the furthest she got with that was naming the last of their four children "Greenleaf Webster" in addition to their first and middle names, but there are so many more things I'd have whispered in Noah's ear, such as, for a start, to re-define the word *mankind* and to use words like *humankind* or *people*, retaining the word *man* to mean "a male person" only, instead of giving it the power to include women, because, while I give him credit for giving us a word for a female person (*woman*), I'd ask why he made it a longer word than *man*, because you'd think he'd have realized that the word *woman* includes *m-a-n*, but *man* does not include *woman*, and I know I'd commend Noah for giving us perfectly good pronouns to use when referring to a man, a woman, and a thing (*he, she, it*) and I'd have encouraged him to keep it that way, but somehow he saw fit to extend the *he* to include *she* (an unfortunate extension), so again, you can see that *she* includes *he*, but *he* does not include *she*, which makes more sense, so if I had been Rebecca Webster sitting alongside Noah during his creative days, I'd have begged him to leave out a whole bunch of words, with the hope they would die natural deaths and not clutter up our language — words such as *bastard, illegitimate, nigger, kike, sissy, tomboy, slut, maid, spinster, hussy* — words that denigrate others, are meant to label, to hurt, to judge, and words we'd be better off without, but what happened, human nature prevailing, was that over time we've given disreputable connotations to some words that began with much nicer meanings, such as Noah's perfectly good words, *queer, gay, bitch, baby, shrew, doll, broad, chick, cow, buck, hunk, hen, dog,* even *mother* (notice how many of those fine words refer to animals), and I'd have asked Noah to skip the words that end unnecessarily in *ess* and *ette*, making special feminine words out of perfectly good nouns — *waiter, actor, bachelor, usher* — and you know that *ess* and *ette* mean "little", and if you doubt, isn't a *cigarette* just a "little cigar", implying that an *actress* is a "little actor" and an *usherette* is a "little usher", and okay, I realize that some women — well, okay, many women — are physically smaller than men, but why blanket all women with a demeaning word that shouts because they are smaller they are worth less than men, but *worthless*, no, I don't believe Noah felt that way, although most men did in those early times and we must thank god that we're smarter now, so perhaps it's time to get down to serious talk that even Rebecca couldn't have foreseen, and that is all about the damage one little four-letter word has come to inflict on women, one little word that has kept women "in their place" for nearly two centuries since Noah Webster first published his dictionary, and of course I don't fault Noah for the oversight since both men and women have twisted the word and used it in ways he could never have guessed, and —oh, the word? — it's *girl*, which sounds harmless, but think a moment, about how adult women who allow themselves continually to be referred to as *girls*, are reinforcing the image of women as childlike, incompetent, irresponsible, weak, and helpless little girls, and what man in his right mind would expect a *girl* to know anything or be able to accomplish anything efficiently, and to make matters worse is that grown women go along with it, giggling and smiling demurely when called a *girl*, perpetuating the image in order to avoid growing up and becoming responsible, competent adults, but that isn't the only damage the words does, and all you have to do is consider another meaning, that because she is "just a girl" she isn't paid on an equal basis with men, or the "other" connotation for *girl* that proliferates the idea of *girls* as arm candy (models or prostitutes), or those supposedly simple-minded women who in reality hold businesses together— secretaries, nurses, teachers, and clerks — and while most of these definitions do not appear in modern Webster dictionaries, some still include the definition of *girl* to include "servant or employee", which sounds the clarion loudly and brashly, that in this twenty-first century we as writers must watch our language closer than anyone else, for as writers, we shape the understanding of words, perpetuate meanings, guide readers, and we don't have to pretend to use beautiful words (*baby, mother, sister*) in order to put down women or anybody else, but choose words carefully, remembering that Noah Webster, and probably Rebecca, simply wrote down the words that already were in use, wrote them as they knew them, not recognizing the power of the sexism that was already ingrained in society through the predominantly male English language, writing words he heard for his first dictionary, a publication which has lasted almost as long as the nation's Constitution (the only one of major countries that still does not included women), causing us to wonder why it has taken us all this time to figure out that women and men share a language as well as life, and that it doesn't have to be lopsided toward male preference, that we don't have to differentiate constantly between women and men, that a *poet* is a poet whether male or female (no need for *poetess*) and that we don't have to lump women together with men in words such as *man, mankind, businessman,* and *manpower,* and… oh, if only I had been Mrs. Rebecca Webster… a wife… a mother… a woman of the early 1800s, would anyone have listened? (1245)

# The Defendant
## by Judy Ashley

*T*HE DEFENDANT SAT IN THE COURTROOM PONDERING how his life had gotten so far out of control in such a short time, but his faith in the American justice system was strong and he knew that he would be exonerated although that did not lessen the overwhelming mental and emotional stress that plagued him and his wife as well as the unwelcome life changes that this terrible ordeal had thrust upon them, including the thousands of dollars they had spent on his legal fees which continued to escalate on a daily basis presenting the probability that he would be forced to declare bankruptcy, which would be unbearable for him since he had always taken pride in paying his debts in a timely manner and maintaining an excellent credit rating that enabled him to purchase his home at a lower interest rate, obtain lower auto insurance premiums, and secure the best credit cards available, all of which contributed to his comfortable middle-class lifestyle that he had worked so diligently to achieve, and now, at the young age of forty-five with a wife and their three children in grade school who would not likely be attending college unless they received a scholarship or could obtain financial aid since he will be broke with a mountain of debts unless he declares bankruptcy, in which case he would be debt free but would lose the family home in the process, and then where would his family live, he wondered as he waited for the jurors to return with their verdict, all the while trying not to let his nervousness be seen by anyone in the courtroom even though his nervousness was certainly justified because the outcome of this trial would change his entire life from now until forever and would also affect the lives of his wife and his children for the rest of their lives as well, but he continued to hold his head high, truly believing that the verdict would be "Not Guilty" because the jury, not being able to ignore the obvious truth, would surely see that he was innocent and would set him free, but at the same time, tiny doubts randomly tiptoed through his thoughts which he immediately pushed away since he had to remain focused on positive thoughts knowing full well that even when the jury finds him "Not Guilty", he would still not be free from the consequences of this entire mess that he had gotten himself into simply by being in the wrong place at the wrong time, because he had played the nice guy doing a favor for a friend, and now he wishes with all his heart that he had gone straight home that night as planned instead of taking his co-worker to that bar on Sunset Drive and then stupidly allowing his friend to talk him into going in with him for *just one beer*, which sounded so good after the stressful day they had at the office, but now he saw how crazy that was especially since he was aware of the bar's reputation and knew full well that entering that establishment was just one big catastrophe waiting to happen and yet, in spite of knowing the risk, he went in for that one cold beer which tasted so good to him before the fight or maybe it was two beers or three (he couldn't actually remember how many beers he had downed) but he sure remembered that bitter aftertaste which made him sick when the fight ended with blood on his shirt and a dead man sprawled on the floor of the bar right there at his feet and oh, it was all so senseless because the fight wasn't about anything important, and anyway he couldn't remember what it was about or what started it, although he did know that it was the worst night of his life since everything began unraveling immediately after that fight, and although he was sure that he wasn't the one who started the fight, he couldn't remember how he even got involved except that his friend appeared to be in trouble and he wanted to help him, but he couldn't remember the details or who threw the deadly punch that took the life of that unknown stranger, which consequently brought him to where he was now, sitting in the courtroom waiting for a jury of his peers to determine the course of his remaining life as if they really knew what happened, or thought they knew, when in reality, all they really knew was what the court allowed to be entered into exhibit or the testimony allowed by the judge when his lawyer objected — after all, they weren't there and he wasn't even exactly sure what happened — but he knew that he could not possibly have thrown that fatal blow because his anger was under control now after completing a few months of intensive anger management therapy, and even if he couldn't remember exactly what happened, his lawyer had done a superb job of defending him and he also thought the prosecutor left quite a bit of room for reasonable doubt, which he was sure the jurors would see and then they would have to set him free, or perhaps they would not be able to reach a verdict, in which case he didn't know what would happen except that it would be problematic since it would leave unsettled doubts in the minds of his family and friends which would most likely destroy what was left of his marriage with his wife getting custody of the children and he would seldom see them, and he had already lost his job because the company found it necessary to replace him due to his thirteen-month absence but, thankfully, the judge had granted bail for which he had to put up his house and most of his liquid assets, including his retirement fund that he had worked so hard to accumulate during the past twenty-five years, all because of one stupid beer stop after work, but it wasn't like he had never stopped for a beer before that particular hellish night, although it certainly wasn't a routine happening for him anymore and now, here he was sitting in the court room waiting to hear the jury's verdict that would determine the outcome of the rest of his life as he desperately attempted to maintain positive thoughts, but when he turned as he looked back at his wife sitting there alone in the courtroom, she looked ten years older as she also waited for the verdict that would determine her future life, and he knew that he was guilty of doing this to her in just thirteen short months, and he had no one to blame but himself because he had brought this horrific scourge down upon the woman he loved, and he wondered if any of it could ever be undone or if there would even be anything left of his life to rebuild when the jury vindicated him, as he realized that his lifestyle would never be the same since his financial portfolio had reversed course, and as he nervously contemplated these things, the jury returned and he slowly rose to stand before the court, hearing the judge ask the jury if they had reached a verdict and the foreman replied, "Yes, Your Honor we have", and while the verdict was handed to the judge, the Defendant solemnly searched the face of each juror, and as he waited for the verdict to be read aloud, the Defendant peered frantically at the judge, took a deep breath, and held it tightly as he heard the verdict echoing throughout the courtroom... (1284)

# Acid Reign
## by Nick Romeo

A BOUT A MONTH AGO I DATED AN IRISH LADY named Rainey O'Blique who I had met at Hades Comet, the club between The Coffee Coffin and Mesquite Bros Seafood Shack in the Southside of Pittsburgh, as she looked amazing that night wearing a fishnet body suit hand-woven from repurposed barbed wire, her purple lips and fuchsia eye shadow accenting her facial muscles, tendons, and blood vessels which were tattooed on her face because she never left home without her red dilated-pupil contacts and duffle bag fashioned from a large carnival teddy bear she won at the *Shoot the Star* booth, reminding me how I took the initiative to approach her with my favorite pick-up line that I made up on the fly, "Excuse me, your name must be Adam, since you are the bomb," which caused us to hit it off wonderfully, after she hit me repeatedly with her brass knuckles, and once my face healed, we went on our first real date, that turned into a circus, and it wasn't that she wore the skin-tight leopard print mini-dress with platform boots which reached above the knees, nor that Rainey fed me popcorn for much of the show while I paid attention to the performances, but it started when she told me she had to use the bathroom and about a half hour later, an announcement came over the loud speaker for everyone to "remain calm and quickly leave the premises" because some of the animals escaped from their cages, and it was then my cell phone rang, and I answered to hear Rainey ordering me to meet her back at the car where I found Rainey sitting in the front seat and a baby tiger in the back, and to my questions she mentioned a friend who runs a conservatory twelve miles away from town, as she lamented that she couldn't fit all the animals in my car and admonished me to buy a bigger vehicle and make sure it's electric powered, and I thought that was the end of Rainey, but later came another memorable date when we went to the museum and dinner, which was the second date and possibly the final one, and this time Rainey wore a translucent white curve-hugging plastic dress with her favorite black platform boots, styling her hair into a Mohawk so tall that she had to duck to get through the door, and needless to say, she caused a multitude of whispers as we toured the exhibits, and resulted in many of the moms covering their sons' eyes, and when she asked me to take pictures of her so she could post them online and update her portfolio, Rainey snuck into the Egyptian exhibit stripped off her dress and covered herself with gauze and posed in King Tut's sarcophagus, and later when we went to the dinosaur exhibit, she climbed up the T-Rex skeleton and positioned herself between the open jaws, still wearing the makeshift gauze dress, and yes, I was able to get some really great shots, along with everyone else standing behind me with their phones until Security finally discovered us when she danced around the modern art room without the gauze dress, holding a megaphone and a can of spray paint, daring the security guards to chase us all over the museum with their Nerf nightsticks and water pistols, resulting in us running through the furniture display, Arctic Room, and hiding in the Hall of Architecture behind a plaster replica of the Pantheon, where Rainey instructed me to create a diversion, which I responded to by running around in circles reciting works by Alan Ginsberg, Democritus, and Mister Rogers until the security guards unsuccessfully tried to grab me just as Rainey jumped out of hiding with her semi-automatic paintball gun that she had concealed in her duffle bag next to the spray paint and megaphone, and opened fire, hitting each guard multiple times in the back, so we left and went to our favorite bar and grill, Dante's Barbeque Inferno, where Rainey reapplied the makeshift gauze dress and we discussed our dreams, goals, and things that we could think about doing one day, to which Rainey told me, "I want to buy Barbie Number One, you know, the first Barbie ever, so iconic," and I asked her why, and she

fired back with, "why do you think?" and I thought for a
moment before telling her, "you want to design a found object
art piece where Barbie is at the center with a bullseye behind
her, signifying the cultural constraints we put on women to
represent an image that is assigned at birth and protected from
dispute," causing her to laugh and tell me No, so I tried again
with, "you want to build a diorama of an ordinary room in a
mundane traditional home and place the Barbie in the middle,
posing suggestively with a Transformer toy from my collection,
or how about Grimlock or Soundwave that would signify the
mechanical nature of the human existence as we are confined
to our domain in relationship to gender roles as dictated by
society," bringing another No, and I finally tried, "you want to
create a short length video where you dress as a terrorist and
have Barbie tied to a normal-size chair and gagged so you can
read a manifesto outlining the plan to cleanse humanity, a kind
of performance art and audio/video installation that would
signify the large and weighty problems affecting women
globally and how so many of these problems, such as unequal
pay, unequal education, and rape culture, are not only ignored
but strongly encouraged," and Rainey paused for several
minutes with her red dilated eyes fully fixated on me, and
finally answered Nah, so I tried one more time with, "okay, you
want to dress as a Navy SEAL and have Barbie dressed as a
terrorist (a news worthy bullet point, get it, bullet point…
SEAL?)" to which Rainey rolled her eyes and put on her brass
knuckles while I continued about how "this would signify the
bondage that women face, as I mentioned earlier, except this
particular expression would investigate how so often women
can be their own worst enemy, making the greater theme about
how all of humanity can be their own worst enemy," where I
referred to a touching scene in the movie "Gods and Generals"
where a Confederate and Union soldier met in a river bed,
chatted briefly, then traded each other a cup of coffee for a
smoke, and once they finished partaking of the shared items,
they went their separate ways… peacefully, the inferrence being

that humanity is too focused on the divisiveness of color, country, gender, and whatever other criteria they use to separate people, to which Rainey unexpectedly quipped that I had been closer with one of my earlier suggestions, to which I begged her to tell me why Barbie Number One was so special, and when she answered that she just liked collecting Barbie dolls and would love to own that first one, I broke off our relationship that night and lived in fear for the next several months, checking underneath my car for bombs, testing the food in my fridge for poisons, and searching the house for booby-traps, getting very little sleep until the day my electric toothbrush almost cut a hole through my cheek, at which time I assumed someone had tampered with it, recalibrating the motor to run a hundred times the normal speed, and another time when I was rushed to the hospital because my body had broken out with pus-filled blisters because someone snuck into my apartment and dipped my blanket and pillow into a mixture of poison ivy, poison sumac, and strychnine, so if you are reading this account, there still might be time to save me, oh yes, this was followed by what I remember as a pretty hand with brass knuckles that placed a rag over my mouth and nose, and I awoke in the trunk of this car, which I think is near the airport because of the sounds I hear, and once I finish writing this letter I will find a way to slide it through this rusted out gap I see in the corner, and I urge you to please get help because I don't know how much time I have…

*Publishers Note*: This letter was found on the side of the road at the entrance to the Pittsburgh Airport and republished after we flushed out misspellings and awkward tenses. Police are still searching for the author whose name has been withheld pending the investigation, but the family has been notified. It is understood that Rainey O'Blique is not her real name, but please contact the authorities if you see anyone who resembles the woman in the only description of her that we could find. We might add that this letter contained numerous gaps in the timeline and discrepancies in the retold experience, causing us to take the liberty to edit and fill in the narrative with our own professional understanding of human nature and criminology. We proclaim ourselves free of any liability. (1531)

# About the Authors
*[The authors of this book are
listed alphabetically by last names,
with page references to their stories.]*

JARED AMOS wrote, "I love this kind of word play that mostly arrives in my head during the night, causing me to leap out of bed and rush to my laptop to write it down before I forget." He is a journalist who works for a news group in DC where he finds plenty of stress as well as a great respect for words. p. 47

DONNA ANDERSON joined the Tacoma Writer's Roundtable after the group published its first anthology in 2000. "I thought maybe I could write well enough to get published, and it turns out I can. The editor of my manuscripts says my sentences tend to become paragraphs; so when I heard about the one- sentence story challenge, that was right down my alley." p. 57

RUTH ANDERSON is a Pacific Lutheran University alumna, retired United States Air Force colonel, and published author. Her career in intelligence included duty in Vietnam, Germany, and Hungary. Ruth has published several works, mostly non-fiction dealing with historical topics. She is also a volunteer tutor of adults learning English. Her submissions for the anthology offered a welcome opportunity to be whimsical. pp. 5, 75, 113

JUDY ASHLEY lives in Lakewood WA with her partner Ed. She has always loved to write. Recently retired from her property management career where her writing was limited to business letters and documents, Judy now writes short stories and poems and enjoys life by participating in a Creative Writing Group, performing with a local theater group, learning to play hand drums, and spending time with her grandchildren. pp. 33, 99, 133

ALLEN BERRY is a 2013 graduate of the Center for Writers at the University of Southern Mississippi. He teaches English at a few colleges around the Huntsville AL area, and has authored three collections of poetry. His fiction has appeared in *Flytrap Uprising* and *The Project*, and his poetry in the *Birmingham Arts Journal*. pp. 4, 37

ROBERTO CARCACHE FLORES is a writer from El Salvador, currently working on his first novel. He mostly writes about his silences, travel, and those rare encounters that make a journey worthwhile. pp. 6, 9

BABZ CLOUGH lives in the Boston MA area and has been a writer for as long as she can remember. She hopes to release her first novel in the coming year and is currently working on a collection of short stories about grief and young widowhood. pp. 30, 43

KELYAN CONN is a pseudonym used by a speech therapist from Texas who admits she has been hired by certain politicians in Washington DC to help them present their public statements so others can misunderstand them. She writes, "I've learned a lot about long sentences. It has become an art." p. 87

ROXANA DAPPER, American English writing activist-educator, has been teaching adult individuals and groups for 20+ years. Her popular workshop presentation, "Do You Suffer from Computer English Disease?" is uncomplicated, entertaining, and immediately useful. She says, "No matter how we re-name hyphens or dashes, they're still roses by any other names." p. 24

DEBBIE DAVIDSON started writing when she was very young and had to wash dishes for the entire family. Because it seemed she'd never finish the task, she would entertain herself by creating stories. She noted, "This challenge, to tell a story in one sentence, was entertaining." p. 63, 91, 109

KIKI DAYTON is a young writer attending college in New England and contemplating a career writing books. She's majoring in psychology with the hope of building strong characters with strong memorable traits. "This is my first published story," she writes. p. 53

VAL DUMOND is owner of Muddy Puddle Press, a linguist, editor, and writer, whose latest book is *American-English: The Official Guide*. She loves to write long sentences, and begins her days by writing out plans for the day in one such sentence. She says it keeps her focused! And relaxed! pp. 61, 121, 129

PATRICK HANKS is a lexicographer, corpus linguist, and onomastician who for ten years was chief editor of the Current English Dictionaries at Oxford University Press. He moved into Academe, and for the past 15 years has held research and teaching posts at universities in America, Germany, Britain, and the Czech Republic. He currently holds two part-time professorships in the UK: at the Research Institute for Information and Language Processing (University of Wolverhampton) and in the Bristol Centre for Linguistics at the University of the West of England in Bristol. (More at: patrickhanks.com.) He was attracted by the challenge of constructing a complete story in a single long sentence as light relief while pondering knotty problems of corpus analysis. p. 30

PAUL JACKSON, a retired Special Librarian and Instructor of Research, an editor/writer, a timpanist and jazz drummer, and chorister, became interested in writing in college when he was paid for his final exam article, and since has published books, articles and essays — including his Carl Sandburg-like sentences. pp. 17, 34, 35

SARA JACOBELLI has worked numerous jobs including dishwasher, bus girl, bartender, newspaper reporter, private investigator's assistant, special education teacher, and librarian. She lives in New Orleans LA and writes fiction and nonfiction. Her work has been published in such places as *Drunk Monkeys Literary Magazine, Bartleby Snopes, First Stop Fiction, Fiction on the Web, The Story Shack, Page & Spine, Postcard Shorts, The New Laurel Review,* and *The New York Times Metropolitan Diary.* p. 51, 97

BILL KAISER is a poet who uses his talent with words to write lyrics for musicians. He currently lives in Nashville TN where he participates in a writers group that is encouraging him to turn his writing into novels. He retains his day job teaching English as a Second Language. p. 77

BONNIE BATEMAN KING holds degrees in Education and Language Arts from Washington State University and in Whole Systems Design from Antioch University, Seattle. She studied art at the Metropolitan Museum of Art (New York City), wrote for a Sydney, Australia magazine, taught memoir writing, is a photographer and writes novels in the Pacific Northwest, enjoying life with her husband Scott, pup Charlie, and elitist cat Riley. p. 22

STANLEY KRIPPNER, PhD, is a professor of psychology at Saybrook University at Oakland CA since 1972, awarded the American Psychological Association Award for Distinguished Contributions to the International Advancement of Psychology for work conducting seminars and workshops around the world. He has authored a very long list of books, his most recent, *The Shamanic Powers of Rolling Thunder* (2016). p.10

DIANE H. LARSON is a retired pastoral counselor and psychotherapist. In addition to journaling her own spiritual journey, she has written poetry, stories, newspaper articles, and has taught classes for fellow travelers on the spiritual path. She is the author of a mystical novel for children of all ages called, *The Kingdom Beyond the Sunset*. pp. 41, 73, 81

LUCIANO MARANO is an author, newspaper reporter, and photojournalist living near Seattle WA. Learn more about his work at www.luciano-marano.com. "I enjoyed the one-sentence story challenge," he said, "because it is the exact opposite of what I do in my news writing work, which demands very concise simple sentences. It's fun to do something so different." pp. 1, 3, 7

DAN MILLS has lived in the Tacoma WA area for over twenty years. After working for Alaska Airlines for thirty-four years, he's looking forward to retirement so he can enjoy his pastimes, writing short stories and oil painting. Says Dan, "Since I learned of the one-sentence story concept, I've had a lot of fun with the exercise." pp. 55, 59

EMILY JAYNE MILTON is a romance writer who says she often gets "stuck trying to solve the triangles that her characters get into" and loves to play word games to get unstuck. She is awaiting publication of her first novel. She writes from her home in Phoenix AZ, where she lives with her husband and young son. p. 45, 49

BETTY MOORHEAD, an 11-year member of a Lakewood WA writers group, has published her book, *To Travel Is To Live* (2013), and now writes extended family stories. She's outlived two husbands, both pilots named Chuck, and a son whose life was destroyed by schizophrenia. This lifetime travel addict has traveled around the world and still has a long bucket list at 86. pp. 83, 85, 89

ANNETTE MUNOZ fell in love with writing at age five and with photography by ten. A third-generation Tacoman, she retired to Arizona after a career in the corporate world. p. 79

CAROL MARGOT NELSON, age 78, wrote this submission in 2012, among 90-odd others, for *The Melrose Mirror.* They were written over a 10-year period for one of the first on-line journals ever. "On thinking it over, most of the nearly 100 articles were… odd," she said. p. 19

NICK PAGE is a Boston-based composer, choral conductor, song leader, and author who does not fish. He likes fish and is not anti-fishing. He simply does not fish. He has written more than a hundred published choral pieces as well as three non-fiction books — none of which are about fish. (Info at www.nickmusic.com.) pp. 13, 32

NITA PENFOLD is a writer/artist digging deep for the taste of the grit and honey in everyday life, creating from the dark currents of the spirit. A graduate of Lesley University's Masters of Arts in Writing program, her poetry has been widely published in anthologies, most recently in *The Absence of Something Specified,* and in the Charters & Charters text book, *Literature & Its Writers* (5th edition). pp. 16, 25, 29

PERRY ANN PORTER, from Poulsbo WA, lives and writes from the beauty spot of the Olympic Peninsula in the state of Washington. p. 14

ANGELA RICHARDSON writes of her entry, "I had this dream when I was about 17, and today I wrote it down for the first time." A transplanted Brit, she writes a sci-fi series for children and a murder mystery series for grownups (her latest, *A Murder at Serenity Farm*) from her rural estate at the foot of the Smoky Mountains in Tennessee. pp. 69, 71

MICHAEL ROBBINS is an outstanding novelist and author of short stories who writes from the heart about the Pacific Northwest. His work draws extensively from mythology, history, and imagination. p. 23

NICK ROMEO is a multidisciplinary artist, musician, and writer. His writings have been published in various literary magazines such as *Uppagus, Nowhere Journal, StreetCake Magazine, Eye Contact, Moonshine Review,* and others. He was interviewed for "Pankhearst's Fresh Featured" of December 2015, "The Dailey Poet Site" of February 2016, *Southern Florida Poetry Journal* of October 2016, and received press on featuredpoet.com in August of 2016. Nick lives in Pittsburgh PA with his wife and their cat, Megatron. pp. 2, 67, 137

JUDE ROY has published widely in such journals and magazines as *The Southern Review, American Short Fiction,* and many others. Originally, from Chatagnier LA, he now works and writes in Madisonville, Kentucky. His collection of short stories *Lighted Windows* is available on Amazon.com as is his mystery/thriller *Searching for Lilith.* pp. 18, 26, 117

TERRY SAGER writes short stories and is working on her first novel, a psychological thriller. Although she often uses humor in her story-telling, she principally writes stories that explore the dark side of the human psyche. When not writing, she volunteers at the local humane society. Terry lives in the Pacific Northwest, with one husband, two dogs, and three cats. p. 107

JENNIFER SCHNEIDER is a life-long learner, online educator, and book lover committed to ensuring all students have every opportunity to achieve their educational goals. She practices, learns, and instructs in the legal, business, and humanities disciplines. She is based in Pennsylvania, U.S.A. and has degrees in Law (J.D.), Economics (B.S.) and Finance (B.S.). pp. 39, 103, 125

JOSH SHORTLIDGE and his wife, now empty nesters, live in Melrose MA, and seek fun and frolic in almost every spiritual and healthy venue that presents itself. He is a database application architect who has other penchants for working with his hands, singing *a cappella*, and crafting decades of Valentine Day extravaganzas. p. 28

RICHARD SILVERMAN has been writing seriously (but not ambitiously) since his mid-30s, ever since he discovered that thinking and word-crafting are what satisfy him most. He's worked as a freelance commercial writer and was published a few times. He now edits for others while remaining an "artist" by nature who writes mostly for himself and for a few online readers who welcome his expressed print. He says, "My writing soothes my soul." pp. 15, 20, 27

JIM TEETERS, MSW, has published poetry in several anthologies. He conducts poetry workshops for children and adults and is active in poetry readings in the Seattle area through the Striped Water Poets. He is the author of seven poetry collections. This "one-sentence story" caught his eye since it was short, like poetry. Jim is a retired social worker living in Kent WA. p. 12

TODD THOMPSON is a poet in New Orleans LA, with a long list of published work, which he says doesn't earn him a penny. He's currently working on a collection of his poetry, which he hopes to publish in a few months. He is a bird watcher, a serious father and grandfather, and enjoys gourmet foods, some of which he cooks himself. p. 65

ELEANOR GRACE WAGNER, of Milwaukee WI, grew up in New England before moving to the midwest where she raised her family. She works as a counselor for Human Services, and writes her stories about the distractions of aging. p. 21

PEGGY ROSE WEBSTER, of University Place WA, is a Korean adoptee committed to becoming the best version of herself from 37-plus years as a wife, entrepreneur (Total Image Solutions), mother of four adult children (one deceased), six grandchildren, and one four-legged fur baby. Amazingly, she located her four half-siblings by age 60, grateful beyond words to be alive and living well. p. 93

KACE WHITACRE, born Kathryn Cecelia Jarvis, uses her name KaCe (pronounced KC) in her life as an artist. KaCe married Jim Whitacre, a fellow student at Western Washington State College, in 1970. She creates custom work in glass, ink on paper for both lettering arts and sumi-e, and jewelry using beads and sterling. She continues to investigate new techniques and media. Reach Kathryn through her website: www.kathryncecelia.com. p. 11

TRONNY WOODBURN is a retired private nurse who loves to write. She heard about this book and thought it would be a perfect way to keep her alert during her long nights sitting up with patients. She now enjoys writing from her beachside home in Mason Springs FL, where she lives with her husband of 43 years. p. 95

BARBARA WYATT writes for many magazines including *Northwest Travel*, *Good Old Boat*, *American Style*, *Boys' Life*, *New York Tennis Magazine* and more. Her new book, *Ode to Tennis* (2017), is a humorous rhyming poem about a recreational player's effort to learn the game of tennis. p. 8

Made in the USA
Columbia, SC
07 January 2020